To Ann & John,

Best wishes for your retirement and we hope this book will bring many memories of your travels in PNG.

Jean & Charlie Codenhead
Shelly & Carl Bailey

IMPRESSIONS
of Papua New Guinea

IMPRESSIONS

of *Papua New Guinea*

TEXT & PHOTOGRAPHY

DAVID KIRKLAND

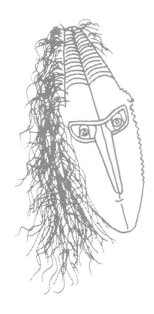

Robert Brown & Associates (Qld) Pty. Ltd.

Designed & published by
Robert Brown & Associates (Qld) Pty. Ltd.
7 Atherton Street
Buranda, QLD. 4102 Australia

© Copyright David Kirkland 1991

Design by Veronica Hughes
Cover design by Glenys Forman
Illustrations by Jada Wilson
Typesetting by Worth Consulting

Distributed in PNG by
Gordon & Gotch (PNG) Pty. Ltd.
P.O. Box 107, Boroko, PNG

National Library of Australia Registry Card No.
and ISBN 1 86273 059 8

Kirkland, David 1958

Contents

Acknowledgements

There are many people I would like to thank who have contributed to the making of this book and the circumstances which led me to write it.

I am particularly grateful to Ted King who hired me and had the courage to turn talk into action and raise the money needed to start what was to become the Foundation for Law Order and Justice. Also Justice Minister Bernard Narokobi who shared with me his vision for Papua New Guinea and the Melanesian people. I would like to thank the people with whom I worked - particularly Violi, Alfred and Tim - who provided support, guidance and friendship, and Sam who gave me an insight into a value system that often sees me questioning my own.

Also thanks to John O'Connor who paid for the port and endured my idealistic tirades when there were few who would listen.

There were many people who encouraged me to see the book completed – particularly my wife and my parents who all know I am prone to starting a new idea a day, without completing the last.

Thank you all for your continued patience.

I would like to thank Jim Tobin who supplied most of my film and photographer Mike McCoy who inspired me to use it. I would also like to thank Jada Wilson for his excellent cartoons.

Above all I would like to thank sincerely the people of Papua New Guinea who were a constant inspiration to my writing and in whose ultimate interest I would like to think this book has been written.

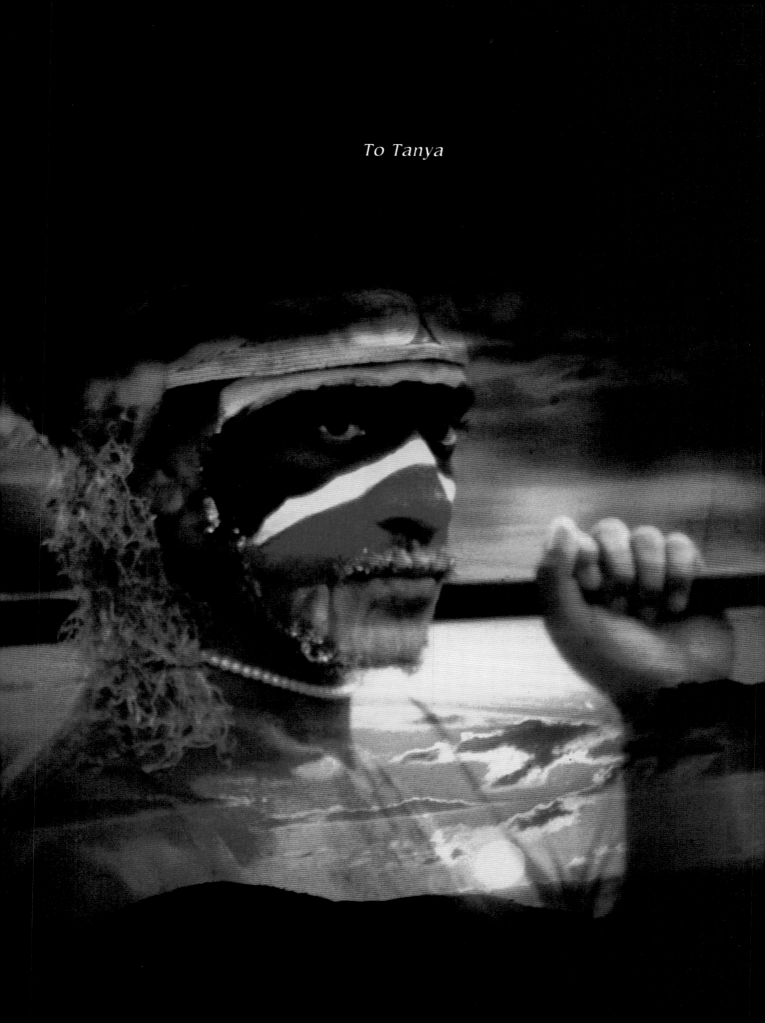

To Tanya

Foreword

"Impressions of Papua New Guinea" is the type of book I wish was available when I arrived in the country.

Like thousands of other visitors, I came to PNG without any real idea of what to expect. I had heard about the tribal fighting and been warned about the lawlessness. I'd been impressed by the clichés – Land of the Unexpected and the World's Last Frontier – and I had seen the pictures of the painted faces and people with bones through their noses. But sadly that's about all I knew of Papua New Guinea and, as I was to quickly discover, there was little in the country apart from time and experience to improve my knowledge.

Ideally, I wanted a book that was both a guide to the country and a point of reference for my own experiences – something light and informative that covered a range of different subjects in a variety of ways. I didn't want volumes of books that I'd have to wade through for snippets of information, or a generally boring autobiography that had no particular relevance to my own circumstance. I didn't want a pretentious coffee table publication to sit on my shelves and gather dust or a tourist booklet that was as illuminating as it was thick. I wanted information, presented in a way that kept me entertained; stories that would give me an insight into attitudes foreign to my own; observations that would credit me with the intelligence to judge their value for myself. I also wanted a pictorial book to capture the attention of a sometimes impatient and unimaginative mind.

So I set about writing it. I had no doubt there was a need for such a book but grave doubts about my commitment to see it finished so I chose a short story format. That way both author and reader could pick it up at whim and pursue the subject of the day, eventually arriving at a collection of impressions that might make a halfway reasonable publication.

I have written about a range of different subjects with no more authority than that of a person who has observed and tried to understand what is happening around him. Where I felt it appropriate, I have added credibility to my ramblings by including more informed opinions.

Although I have endeavoured to provide a balanced and honest interpretation of what I have experienced in my time here, I confess there has been the odd occasion when I have erred in favour of providing an entertaining account rather than a Hansard's report (The product of my all too serious training as a journalist). I would like to add, however, that I have not done the same when referring to matters relating to crime in this country as my position has made me uniquely aware of the temptation for people to sensationalize the situation. Sadly, the law and order problem is a dominant aspect of urban life in PNG and it cannot be overlooked.

In short, this book has been written for people who see their time in Papua New Guinea as an opportunity to learn more about both this country and themselves. It is those people who will understand that what has been written is not a definitive statement about Papua New Guinea but simply an introduction to a host of subjects about which they are invited to draw their own conclusions.

David Kirkland
Author

Above: Early morning mist rises from the cold, damp peat of the goldfields of Mt Kari. Panning begins at first light and continues until the sub-zero temperatures drive the villagers back inside their smoke filled humpies.

Right: Despite the freezing temperatures of the Mt Kari goldfields, traditional dress is common. New found wealth provides for western luxuries such as umbrellas, pans and shovels.

FIRST IMPRESSIONS

ARMY RIOT – GOLDFIELD UPRISING
FIRED AT BY WARRIORS.

It was an eventful introduction to my new job in Papua New Guinea. While I was settling into my house and a 12 month contract, hundreds of disgruntled soldiers were marching on Parliament House protesting for higher salaries and better conditions. Cars were overturned and property damaged.

Expatriate opinion about the incident the next day provided little comfort, with stories about the general extent of the country's law and order problems running rampantly in the minds and from the mouths of the people around me. Corruption at all levels of government; rascal gangs that roam the country's urban centres day and night raping and pillaging. In the highlands, tribal warfare raged unabated while throughout the country both nationals and expatriates lived behind barbed wire fences, some with surveillance systems, dogs and 24 hour security guards.

".......So what did you say you were doing here?"

I had been recruited from Australia to Port Moresby to co–ordinate a national awareness campaign aimed at reducing crime in Papua New Guinea. The government had given law and order a top priority and the private sector decided to bring in someone with public relations experience to support and encourage the government's initiatives.

What qualified me for such a job I hear you ask. Well, apart from my media experience, probably very little. I had just finished a consultancy in the Pacific country of Vanuatu which ended abruptly when the minister I was advising on marketing the country as a tourist destination decided he wanted to overthrow the government. Not a good move according to the Australian government which was paying my way, so that ended rather abruptly. My 12 months experience in a developing Pacific country and a blinding reference which I drafted myself did, however, give me some advantage over the rest of the field.

It was four months earlier, I first set foot in Papua New Guinea. I was on a working holiday in the Pacific and decided to visit the highlands. Exercising one of the privileges of one of my previous professions, I jumped into a helicopter bound for the goldfields of Mt Kare in the Southern Highlands Province to have a look at what had become the country's biggest national goldrush. At the time, it was more a joy ride than a serious intention to write something for the papers back home and certainly floating 4,000 ft over cloud tipped mountains was a welcome change to travelling in the back of a highland PMV (local bus).

However, expectations of comfort were quickly shattered as we prepared to land near the geologist camp at which I was a guest. In the valley below, hundreds of landowners with machetes and axes were charging up the hill like something out of "Zulu Dawn".

Regrettably, neither my hysteria nor any amount of money could persuade the helicopter pilot to desert the camp and return me to the comfort of the PMV, so we landed. The moment we touched down, clouds of tear gas exploded nearby as police helicopters swooped from the skies. There was chaos as the wailing crowd shrieked and retreated back

Above: In a demonstration by soldiers over pay conditions, protesters commandeered trucks and paraded through the main streets in convoy, smashing and looting shops as they moved forward.

Right: The amount of alluvial gold found at Mt Kare was staggering. Ten year old children arrived at the scales with coffee jars full of gold pebbles while others turned up with nuggets the size of their fist.

Below: Hawkers were plentiful in the goldfields, selling everything from hot chicken soup and watches to whisky and women. Their charges were exorbitant, five to 10 times the purchase price, though the demand for luxuries was always high.

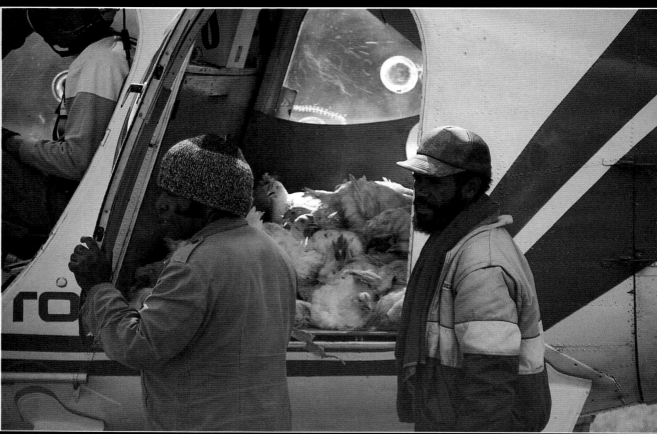

Above: Children were valued in the goldfields for their keen eyes. Squatting in the ice-cold mud in bare feet, they would spend all day picking through the mud in search of alluvial gold.

Left: The women tirelessly carted the mud in panning plates on their heads, while the men and children sieved through it looking for the gold.

Opposite Bottom: Helicopters charging $400 a round trip were used by the hawkers to ferry live chickens into the Mt Kare goldfields. A constantly boiling stew with an aroma that wafted down into the valley guaranteed customers eager to part with their gold.

down into the valley.

I spent a long, cold night listening to the campfire catcalls below while the geologists told me about the problems the new wealth had brought to the area. Landowners were entitled to whatever alluvial gold they could find and hundreds of fortune hunters had migrated into the area. Subsistence farmers still dressed in "ass grass" were pulling out hunks of gold the size of their fist and finding themselves with more money than they knew what to do with. They travelled to nearby Tari, a frontier town, looked at what others were doing with their wealth and did likewise. Apart from devouring truckloads of local luxuries such as Twisties and Coca Cola, they bought video players and television sets for their villages, not realising they needed electricity to run them. Cars were also purchased and abandoned less than a day later, with owners assuming their usefulness expired at the end of a tank of petrol.

Back in the goldfields, hawkers sold everything from tents and hot food to cigarettes and wrist watches. Helicopters, charging $400 a trip, were chartered to bring in live chickens. A constantly boiling pot of broth and a wafting aroma that covered half the valley ensured a constant clientele and little resistance to the exorbitant charges. Come nightfall, contraband alcohol, prostitution and gambling provided temporary relief to long hours of toil in the ice cold peat. Along the tracks out of the valley bandits waited for those who had found good fortune but had run out of luck.

As we made our way back to Tari the next day palls of smoke could be seen in the distance. According to the pilot, tribal fighting was common in the region and the smoke was likely to have been caused by a raiding party. Ten metres beneath us lay the charred remains of a small village. The huts had been burnt, crops had been uprooted and no one was in sight. We lowered the helicopter so I could take a closer photograph.

In the following few seconds I came to despise my camera as it brought into focus a circumstance I could certainly have done without. Directly in front of us about 20 warriors in war paint, shields and all the trimmings were firing arrows at us from the clearing, several ricocheting from the cockpit. It was a predicament that saw me as calm as any hysterical passenger could be, believing one arrow in the rotor was all it would take to see us plummeting earthward. My concern, however, was to multiply still further when I realised my pantomime screams were being drowned out by the shrieking pilot next to me who had all but frozen at the controls. The helicopter was spinning like an off centre gyroscope. The warriors beneath us were scattering for cover.

Not good I surmised.

Predictably, my voice returned with a pitch and force that could have powered the helicopter on its own and fortunately it was enough to shake the pilot from his stupor. Shakily, we continued towards our destination.

If nothing else I have had a varied introduction to this country. In less than three weeks in PNG I had been in the middle of a goldfield uprising, been fired at by highland warriors and survived the aerial antics of some lunatic who should be peeling potatoes in an aerial academy. To mark my return to Papua New Guinea, the army had run amok, the politicians are dividing the country and the rascals are raping and robbing more people than ever.

It promises to be an interesting 12 months.

Above: Entire families were involved in the search for gold. They would trek from their villages well down in the valley and live for weeks in dank, sub-zero conditions with little water or food apart from what they traded for their gold.

Left: Suddenly there were warriors firing arrows at us from the bushes, several ricocheting off the helicopter's cockpit.

Top, Centre & Bottom: To eat the Betelnut, you break open the husk with your teeth and chew on the soft inner flesh, then add some lime and bite on a mustard stick. The result comes quickly - the dizzying rush, the perspiration, then the telltale grin.

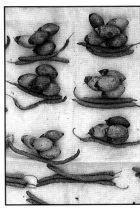

Far Left, Centre & Left: Betelnut is very much a part of the social process in Papua New Guinea. A reported 180,000 a day are consumed in the national capital alone. For many nationals, Betelnut is the only source of income. Villagers will travel great distances to the cities to lay a piece of hessian on the ground near a popular walkway and sell their betelnut. Like good restaurants, many sidewalk Buai sellers have regular customers.

BETELNUT: BUAI

THE ATTRACTION – HOW TO EAT IT – WHEN IN ROME – BBC JOURNALIST SWEARS NEVER AGAIN

Chewing Betelnut nut, or Buai (boo–eye) as it's called in the local lingo, is a national pastime. It's as common as smoking in any other country, only instead of being inhaled, it's chewed and instead of blowing it out as smoke, what's left is spat out, arriving where it lands as a congealed red mass of fibre and fluid. Betelnut shares many of the drawbacks related to smoking. It stains (fingers, teeth, concrete and pant legs), it's addictive (though many who eat it would deny the fact) and it's abhorred by most who don't indulge. ("vulgar, filthy habit"). Nationals who chew it regularly swear by it, while the few expatriates who have tried it tend to swear about it. It costs about 50 cents a nut and many who can afford it chomp up to a dozen a day, some two at a time. Though there is no age limit to starting, like smoking, kids are imitating their parents at about 13.

Buai is highly regarded throughout both Asia and the Pacific. Records of its consumption in Asia date as far back as China's Tang Dynasty (618AD) when it was sent annually to the imperial court as a delicacy. In the country today, the nut represents a billion dollar industry, with plans to can, freeze and dry it for export around the world.

The actual nut is the shape of a large acorn, green or yellow in colour. It can be a stimulant, responsible for increased concentration and energy, or it can make you dizzy and nauseous – depending on the strength of the Betelnut and fortitude of the recipient. According to PNG connoisseurs, it's an excellent substitute for thirst and hunger, the husk makes a good tooth brush, and sharing it is a great way of meeting people ("G'day mate, let me buy you a Buai!"). It is commonly used to cement peace negotiations and is an important ingredient in sorcerer's potions. Recently the establishment of a Ministerial Buai Club was tabled on the agenda in Parliament and though consumption was banned in the corridors of power, it's eating has been encouraged behind closed doors. A special task force has been created to investigate its export potential for medical and social purposes. Whatever the qualities or drawbacks, buai is popular. In the national capital alone, a reported 180,000 are consumed a day and increased consumption of the nut has been held solely responsible for the country's CPI blowout.

It goes without saying that most curious people are likely to "Kai–Kai the Buai" (a popular song title) if the opportunity presents itself so last night

I sampled it for the first time. It was a clandestine circumstance, sort of like school days when the oldest in the group would buy cheap wine and we'd all sneak behind a bush and get legless. Expatriates, we were told, simply don't eat Betelnut.

John, an English radio journalist I had met a week earlier, and I drove through town at night until we found someone who had some Betelnut for sale. Fearful that we would collapse where we ate, we went back to my place to divide the booty (half a nut each being the extent of our daring). Said our supplier: "Why do you want it? It will only make you crazy."

As in the days of my youth, further encouragement was not needed.

The ritual begins by breaking open the Betelnut with your teeth, chewing the soft inner flesh ("This is bloody horrible") and sticking it behind your gums on one side of your mouth ("Whose idea was this?"). It is brittle and similar in taste to a chalky banana.

After a few quick chomps you take a mustard stick (called Daka) and dip it in lime powder –both are generally sold with the Buai – also adding it to your mouth. It's the lime that turns the nut bright red.

Reaction to the Betelnut can take two distinct courses. Both are immediate. You can get a mild rush, feel high and come down all in the space of time it takes you to chew it or you can – as John discovered – become violently ill.

Let me delight, as I have done several times since, in recounting John's experience.

At first we just sat and looked at each other testingly, waiting for a sign. Then we began to sweat profusely. A dizzying rush came on, there was a giggle, a murmur of recognition and as quickly as it came, it was over – at least for me.

At the other end of the couch, however, sweat continued to drip from John's face, only it looked like someone had turned on a hidden faucet. His complexion had gone deathly white, his head was flung back with mouth agape and his eyes were intensely focused on some obscure point on the ceiling.

"Are you OK John?" (It was more curiosity than sympathy. I was shrieking with laughter).

Silence.

Suddenly he was up on his feet and heading towards the doorway. I say towards because he passed over several pieces of furniture and through the flyscreen to get there.

What amazed me was he managed to maintain his BBC voice as he went. Despite his obvious disorientation, he denied anything was wrong. "....Fine,.... just need a little air ..... tea would be nice."

With that, he disappeared into the darkness, fell down the stairs, crashed into the garden and set about decorating the landscape with a commitment of force and volume that silenced even the neighbourhood dogs.

He was outside a good 10 minutes before he briefly reappeared on the verandah.

"Won't be a sec..... Terribly sorry about this ...... how's the teaaaaaggggggghhhhhhhh!"

Gone again.

Poor guy. I shan't go on. Needless to say, he survived the ordeal and spent the next day apologising for the demon that possessed him. He claimed it was an empty stomach that caused his illness but that seems doubtful. Certainly the garden he levelled the night before told a different story.

Personally, I'd recommend everyone tries Betelnut at least once. It's harmless (at worst, no more harmful than a heavy night on the grog), it provides an interesting cultural insight and, if nothing else, it's great entertainment on an otherwise quiet Friday night in Papua New Guinea.

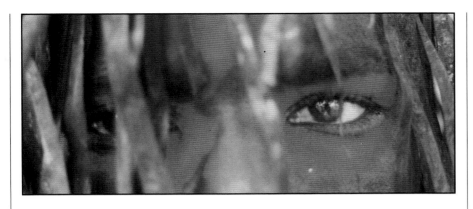

Left: Rascal stories abound in the capital cities, with the extent of the crimes varying, depending on who you ask. Horror stories circulate the expatriate community like wildfire, often as embellished versions of the truth made into entertaining dinner conversation. As a rule, newcomers are best to qualify what they hear, rather than naively accept what they have been told.

SECURITY

LIVING BEHIND BARS
RAIDING RASCALS – EYEWITNESS ACCOUNTS.

If I had any doubts about the extent of the law and order problem in Port Moresby, my accommodation in the hill suburb of Gordon has done little to allay the concern. Twenty four hour security guards are stationed at the entrance of the fenced compound. In each of the 20 units, bars cover the windows, steel security screens open onto double deadlock doors and electronic surveillance systems monitor the interior with infa–red beams. Each house has a direct telephone line to the security office. Dogs patrol the perimeter.

Overkill? You would think so until you talk to some of the compound residents. Many who stay here say they wouldn't live anywhere else. They pay in excess of K500 (AUD $750) a week for the privilege, though most, like me, are company sponsored.

By any standards, this compound is considered one of the more secure in Port Moresby. Generally, most expatriate settlements are surrounded by barbed wire fences and have security guards. In fact you're unlikely to see any suburban home without barbed wire fencing or security across the windows.

It's a strange situation, residing in a foreign country and yet living in a circumstance so detached from it. From my balcony I can look out across the pristine compound grounds through the fence and into the neighbouring suburb. I can see kids playing on the roads and women carrying bilum bags swollen with vegetables. Nothing you can see seems threatening, yet in reality no one on either side of the fence would deny the need for having it.

After only three weeks, I will not try to assess the threat of living in Port Moresby, however, one story (and three versions) of a recent incident where rascals breached compound security, provides an interesting insight.

Person One: (Pilot, early 40's, moved in to the compound recently out of concern for his family)

"There is always someone getting robbed, beaten or raped. Just last week a gang of rascals cut their way in through the back fence and broke into the house on the hill. There was about 15 of them, armed with guns and knives. Both the husband and wife were inside along with their two children. They put a shotgun to his head and raped the wife with a knife to her throat while the kids were watching. Meanwhile, an expatriate

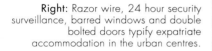

Right: Razor wire, 24 hour security surveillance, barred windows and double bolted doors typify expatriate accommodation in the urban centres.

returning home was driving through the security gate when one of the guards stopped him and told him not to go up there as it was too dangerous. Ignoring the guard's warning, the expatriate screeched up to the house in time to see the rascals running off with a video, sound system and jewellery. If I had been there I would have shot the bastards."

Person Two: (Housewife, mid–thirties)
"I heard the whole thing and spoke to the woman afterwards. It must have been terrifying. Seven rascals were kicking and punching the husband and two were holding knives to their children's throats while the other four had the wife on the floor with her pants down. I heard her screaming and called the security guards. The rascals panicked and ran, taking all the family valuables. I keep my doors well bolted all the time. It could happen to any one of us."

Person Three: (Geologist, mid–30's, father of five)
"It was a band of four kids – no more than 15 years old – with knives. They cut a hole in the back fence and waited in the garage for the family to come home. While the man was parking the car, two of them grabbed the woman and tried to force her up the stairs to rape her. The two others got into a fight with the man, but when they realised they weren't having any luck with either, they took off, taking a telephone and a referdex. I heard some woman screaming and chased two of them away. It was over in less than five minutes. They were just bored kids. I never lock my door and I've never had any problems. It's all a matter of attitude."

NOTE: I did not speak with the people involved as the incident happened a month earlier and they had left by the time I arrived.

HOUSE MERI

GLOWING REFERENCE – COLONIAL ATTITUDE
KEYS TO THE HOUSE – DOMESTIC BLISS.

It's been two weeks since I hired Winnie to give me a hand with the domestics. She just materialized on my doorstep one morning like some abandoned waif. Short, stocky, middle aged and standing in bare feet, she wore a floral pattern Mother Hubbard with a hat that matched her multi–coloured bilum. In one hand she trailed a basset–eyed infant, in the other, a letter of introduction. I got the impression she had been waiting since first light but she certainly didn't make it obvious.

As I stepped from behind the flyscreen door sprouting the only two words of greetings in Pidgin I knew, Winnie giggled and handed me the folded piece of paper. She continued to shuffle her feet in apparent embarrassment, eyes never leaving the ground. "Mi gudpela meri, mi klenim ol haus bilong yu," she muttered.

The letter was a glowing reference from the previous occupant.

In Port Moresby, domestic help is commonplace among expatriates as labour is so cheap. Some frown upon it as a legacy of the colonial era but those who can afford it prefer to think they are keeping locals at work. Me, I'm just lazy – effective time management I call it. As I did back home, I will pay anyone whatever it costs to absolve me from domestic purgatory.

So Winnie's prospects are looking good and she can sense it. Excitedly she bursts into a list. "Mi wasem floa na dis, pressim clos, klinim ples waswas....." Whatever she was saying it sounded too good to pass up and, after considerable negotiation (sign language doesn't allow for hasty settlement), we agreed on two days a week (the turnabout period for my wardrobe). Pay would be 25 Kina ($40) a fortnight – the going rate according to others in the compound, though Winnie assured me she was previously paid twice that.

The next day I handed Winnie the keys to the house and left her to it. In retrospect, I shouldn't have assumed that because she nodded enthusiastically at everything I said, she'd understood anything I was saying.

When I returned at the end of day one, Winnie had been and gone. She had taken everything that wasn't tied down and hidden it in places I am yet to discover. In the bathroom, she had used an entire $23 bottle of Le Tan moisturizing milk to wipe down the walls, toilet, bathtub and sink. In the kitchen her dedicated effort with the steel wool saw most of the Teflon scraped off my new set of non–stick cookware and in the loungeroom my only Playboy magazine had mysteriously disappeared to be replaced by a watchful photograph of my fiancee. She had disinfected the floors with lime cordial, dusted to a level no higher than her reach (the rooms looked like they had a two metre high–tide mark) and my weekend newspapers – unread and treasured – had gone.

When I mentioned all this to Winnie when next she arrived, she again burst into a series of enthusiastic nods, although this time their meaning was blatantly apparent... ....she didn't understand a word I was saying!!

Today, I am happy to report we have overcome most of the initial hurdles. I speak a little more Pidgin and Winnie has become a little more accustomed to my sub–human domestic habits. Although large quantities of soap powder keep disappearing and my clothing often smells like it has been washed in with a dozen ancient Bilums and half the village laundry, generally our partnership is working out pretty well.

Right: Elaborate headdresses created from hundreds of bird feathers are meticulously prepared. Each feather is carefully unwrapped from paper and packed boxes, then placed in the headdress to ensure the highest possible standards of presentation.

Above: Sogeri is located on a 600 metre plateau which overlooks Port Moresby. The drive from the capital along the Loloki River Gorge, provides a spectacular view of the waterfall that spills from the mountain water catchment.

Right: The Bilas is made from both natural and man made accessories. Leaves and flowers are obviously favoured because of their availability, while some of the more elaborate bilas are made from rare bird feathers and carved pieces of bone.

SOGERI SING SING

PORT MORESBY SHOW – THE RIGOS VERSUS THE HIGHLANDERS – STUDENT SUCCESS.

It was a disappointing turn–out in the traditional dancing section at the Port Moresby Show this year. Instead of 23 groups turning up in the colour and finery of their traditional Bilas as they did last year, only eight and a half arrived. Good as they were, it was not the same. "We thought they would fill the arena," said a national onlooker.

Unfortunately tribal rivalry can influence the annual shows and sadly this year the Rigo tribe from the Papuan region threatened several highland clans with violence if they turned up. As a result, more than half the groups that were expected stayed at home – including the Rigos.

For most expatriate onlookers there was little to indicate it was anything less than a normal Port Moresby Show. There were the crowds (about 120,000 people) the stalls, the food halls, the exhibitions and the entertainment. In the traditional dancing arena there were at least two of the groups many had come to see –the Huli wig men with their hats of human hair and the Mekeo dancers with their striped yellow faces and elaborate feather headdresses.

However, for those with a point of comparison, the traditional dancing lacked the grandeur of past performances. It was a parade without a band, a circus without the clowns.

Some three weeks later, murmurs of another Sing Sing drifted down from the mountain plateau near Sogeri, about 45 minutes out of Port Moresby. There was no great mention about it in the tourist calendar. A few handbills appeared in shop windows. The week before, the newspapers ran a couple of stories focusing on the fact that for the first time in the 13 year history of the event the venue had been changed from Konedobu Cultural Centre to Sogeri High School. From afar it had more the air of a school fete than a significant cultural event.

By 9.30 in the morning the preparation area outside the main arena was a flurry of activity. Around small permanent huts representing different regions – the Sepik, the Eastern Highlands, the Western Highlands, New Guinea Islands, Milne Bay, Northern Province, Central Province, Chimbu and Enga – young men and women were adorning themselves with paints and feathers. It was not like the Port Moresby Show where many groups turned up in trucks already prepared for the dancing. Here you were able to watch the care and precision that went into each costume. You could move between the people to take photographs and get close enough to smell the coconut oil and the ochre paints as they were applied. You could see the delicate unwrapping of the Bird of Paradise feathers, the discipline that went into setting the costumes and the attention that was focused on traditional detail.

Around the Central Province hut the Mekeo students sat patiently in front of their elders as thin stripes of yellow and orange paint were meticulously applied with pieces of leaf. Old women with tattooed faces mothered their daughters, correcting and re–correcting their headdresses, lovingly grooming their hair. In the Eastern Highland section young men borrowed bright red paints from Chimbus to smear their bodies while others from the Sepik shredded bamboo sticks into headdresses and skirts. The girls sat in restless anticipation, waiting for parents to complete the final touches.

Above: The Port Moresby Show - a cultural, agricultural and industry showcase - is one of the most popular events in the national calendar. Thousands of spectators from throughout the Central Province converge on the nearby showgrounds.

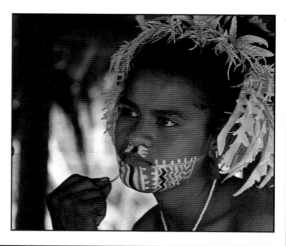

Right & Below: The Mekeo girls from the Central Province are easily recognised by the bright yellow lines painted onto their faces. Leaves and feathers were used to apply the paints

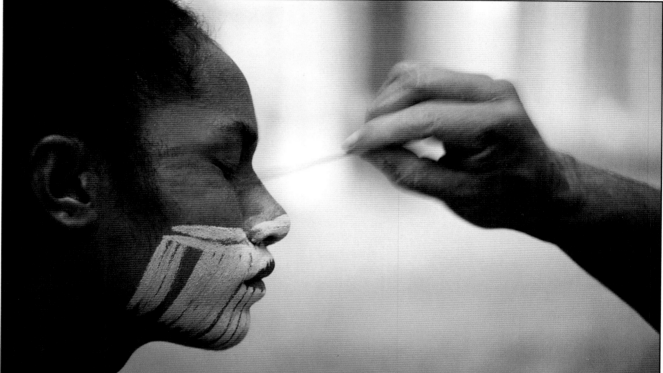

Of course there was competition as each group tried to outdo the other but it was all done in a spirit of fun and friendship. For those who were a long way from home, the Sing–Sing was an important opportunity to share their knowledge and take pride in their culture.

And then the culmination of hours of effort. Each group was given a number by which it would move into the arena. One by one they filed in, parading around the perimeter to the applause of the audience. Outside, while each group waited to be called, the others continued to rehearse their dancing, synchronising their movements and pounding their Kundu drums. As one group completed their parade, another came in –17 in all – winding up the day at about four o'clock with all the students gathered in the arena to the applause of the crowd.

It was heartening to see the success of the Sogeri Sing Sing and the attitude of the students that participated. The performers thoroughly enjoyed themselves, almost as much as the spectators.

Even those with a point of comparison thought it was an excellent day.

Far Left: There was a charming innocence about the students and the pride with which they demonstrated their culture.

Left: Mothers lovingly groom their daughters for the Sing Sing, watchfully chaperoning them through the excitement of the day.

Below: In an air of excitement and anticipation, the Mekeo girls are decorated by their elders with a painstaking detail that takes several hours. As much importance is placed on the preparation of the dancers, as their actual performance.

Right: Students from the Sepik River took part in the Sogeri Sing-Sing, preparing inside a hut decorated to look like a Haus Tambaran.

Below: The faces of the young Mekeo men are also painted with striking colours and crowned with elaborate feather headdresses.

Above: The Tolai whipping ceremony of East New Britain in which young boys stand or kneel and have their limbs flogged by long vines as a test of manhood. Remarkably, the boys barely grimace, despite several blows that have onlookers at the Sogeri Sing Sing cringing.

Top Left & Top Centre: There were moments in the camera when the young men were transformed into adults only to be returned to their innocence by a giggle or a gesture they were unable to contain.

Left: The day took on a theatrical dimension as young teenagers combined different elements of their culture into the presentation. This young man, though painted with Sing Sing colours and adorned in feathered headdress, carries a fighting spear more likely to be seen on the shoulders of a camouflaged highland warrior.

SUDDEN IMPACT

LASTING DAMAGE

One of the saddest aspects of living in a developing country is watching it innocently mimicking the mistakes of the western world.

In many ways a new nation is like a petulant child. It demands what others have, with little regard for the cost; it duplicates what it sees, without knowing what it really looks like.

There is little doubt that expatriates are a role model for many of the young in this country. You can see it in the way they dress, hear it in the way they talk and feel it in the way they relate to you. They want what expatriates have and unfortunately, sometimes unwittingly, we pass onto them the worst of what we have to offer.

Last night Clint Eastwood's movie 'Sudden Impact' was playing at the local theatre. For two hours a stadium full of impressionable teenagers were glued to scenes of graphic violence, frontal nudity, swearing and brutal rape.

In a country where government and police are struggling to convince people still coming to terms with a basic education that violence is bad, our hero was punching women in the face, condoning murder and abusing police authority. Arguably it may have its place in a modern world where people understand the difference between the movies and real life, but in a developing country it promises only tragedy to the future.

"What did you like most about the movie?" I asked a 13 year old boy during interval.

"I thought it was great when he smacked that woman to the ground," he said.

This country has a censorship board, in fact just recently it fined a tourist for trying to bring a picture of a naked woman into the country. Regrettably, however, like many fledgling organisations in Papua New Guinea, it is overworked and understaffed.

It's a sad fact that enforcement of censorship standards will remain a low priority in the context of this country's ambition to become a modern nation. Sad because the questionable moral standards being set by western example are likely to continue to have not just a sudden impact, but a lasting impact on the attitudes of Papua New Guinea's youth.

Opposite page: There are thousands of great movies in the world that offer an abundance of beauty, humour and entertainment, yet violent and sexually explicit movies continue to be imported and screened in theatres throughout PNG. It is a sad fact that enforcement of PNG's censorship standards is likely to remain a low priority in the context of the country's ambition to become a modern nation.

SAM

A VISIT TO HIS VILLAGE – OBSERVATION – SPECIAL PERFORMANCE – VILLAGE VALUES – RETURN HOME

Sam and I are about the same age and currently occupy roughly similar positions, though he is a national working with the government and I am an expatriate funded by the private sector. We arrived at our respective positions along two very different paths. While I was struggling to become a journalist back in Australia, Sam had left his village and joined the armed services. When I moved into public relations Sam left the army and returned to his village. About six months ago a chance meeting saw him offered a job by Justice Minister Narokobi. About the same time I responded to an advertisement in a national newspaper in Australia.

Today Sam is the senior co-ordinator of the government's Law and Order Secretariat and I am the Chief Executive of the Foundation for Law Order and Justice. Brought together as counterparts in a national campaign to improve the country's law and order standards, we have spent a lot of time together.

Recently Sam and I had cause to go to Lae as part of a tour to establish law and order offices in the Morobe and Highland provinces and while we were there I visited Sam's village. It was about a half hour journey along a pock marked, unsealed road. As we travelled through the rainforest terrain Sam recounted stories of some of the families in the area. He talked at length about their history and of their relationship with neighbouring clans –stories passed down to him through the generations by his "Granny" or grandfather, one of the community's great orators. We frequently pulled over, some times to give people a lift, though mostly so Sam could introduce me to "Big men" (respected leaders) along the way. Though there was no explanation, it was apparent the gesture was welcomed. Everyone we spoke to warmly took my hand and wished us well.

"Everything on this side of Markham River is the land of the Wampur people," said Sam with pride.

"As far as you can see, it's been my family's for generations. My land is in those hills – one day I will build a house and grow taro.....and here is my village."

Before us was a cluster of ramshackle timber houses haphazardly arranged on parched ground the size of a football field. The abundance of timber was unusual compared to most villages I had seen but, as Sam pointed out, there were benefits to having a saw mill – a joint venture between the community and the provincial government – located a few kilometres away. Most of the houses were of basic design, rectangular shells of weather worn planks. Some were on stilts, no glass in the windows, no fences or boundaries. Pigs wallowed in the nearby shade while dogs patrolled the dusty corridors scavenging for morsels. Like Gothic gargoyles, old men squatted in darkened doorways scrutinising the daylight. Children playfully raced after one another scattering panicked chickens and piglets into clouds of dust.

As we parked the car and walked towards the central meeting place, curious faces emerged from the shadows.

"Say Boanu," whispered Sam. "It means good morning."

The gesture sent shrieks of delight through the village.

Eventually we arrived at where the elders sat – a dim, sheltered area, hazy with campfire smoke. Several old men and women sat around the

Opposite Page: Sam and his family at Wampur Village. He would take every opportunity to return to his village where life he said was so simple and uncomplicated. "The village is where my roots are – I was born here and I will die here. Being in offices is like wearing shoes – I never really feel comfortable in them."

Right: Sam in traditional attire: "I'll be dancing at the Port Moresby Show with people from my village. We have been practising ever since the day we were born."

smouldering fire and rose to meet me as we walked in trailing scores of still curious faces. In turn they all moved to shake my hand and welcome me to their village. An area of ground was cleared for me to sit on and the milling crowd of children was told to stand back. Dogs were chased out of sight.

As Sam talked about the purpose of our visit, the group paid him the attention of a big man, mesmerised by stories of life in the capital. Bananas and buai were passed around. As I bit into the husk and dipped the mustard stick in lime, Sam delighted: "By tomorrow everyone will be talking about the white man who ate betel–nut in our village," he said.

While Sam continued to speak, young boys gathered around to talk to me and practise their English. I thought about what it must be like for them to live here without many of the western comforts which I tend to take for granted.

In the village there are no free medical benefits or unemployment handouts. Those who fall sick endure it or depend on traditional medication such as sorcery. Those without salaried work become farmers, hunters and foragers of food.

It was apparent that time – so much a pre-occupation of the western world – was largely irrelevant, measured not in hours and minutes but at best day and night. With no deadlines to meet, no frantic rushing around, everyone has the time to talk to one another and share in their common circumstance. In the distance young children shrieked as they leapt from a branch into a nearby river while a group of older boys tirelessly chased a football. It all seemed so incredibly simple and generally everyone appeared remarkably content.

Probably the only restless group was some young men who had just left school. They had been taught much and were obviously impatient to use what they had learnt. It was sad to realise many would soon head for the big towns – lured by tales of wealth and adventure – only to find a world far more hostile than anything they could imagine.

While we were there I met Sam's family, his wife and five young children whom he hadn't seen in more than three months. "It is very difficult," he said when I commented on the separation.

"I feel I should be with them and here to help my village."

That afternoon a special dance and drama performance was put on, with Sam and myself as the guests of honour. Once again food was shared – oranges, bananas, rice and chicken. I watched as those around me revelled in the simple pleasures of the day, supremely comfortable on the grass in the shade, completely absorbed by the performance. There were no bright colours or theatrical props, though by the audience's reaction, it could have been a command performance. They loved it. There was a lot to see and so much more Sam wanted to show me. "This is the tree where our young prepare for battle, this is where our forefathers first settled the village."

As our two weeks together progressed I learnt more about the customs and beliefs of Sam's village and was given an insight into a wealth often overlooked in the western world.

It is in villages such as Sam's, amid the apparent poverty, the true Melanesian character has evolved – so very different from what is seen in urban centres such as Port Moresby. As Sam pointed out, it is characterised by the people's tremendous affinity to their land and their loyalty to their community.

Generally, everyone in the village is entitled to land either by direct inheritance or marriage says Sam.

"All the men have their own land from which they can grow food and get materials to build a house," he said.

"From an early age men and women are taught to work the soil so they can survive. They learn about the spirits of our ancestors and the responsibility that comes with ownership."

According to Sam it is not like Australia where people buy and sell their property without a second thought. "Our land is part of us; we were born on it and we will die in it. It is like a parent in whom we have complete trust. We may leave it for some time but we will always return.....and be welcomed," he said.

Sam says that it is from this attachment that there has evolved a tremendous sense of belonging and community spirit.

"In Papua New Guinea we call it the Wantok system, where community members are obligated by tradition to assist one another above all else – even the law. It means no one member of the community will go hungry while there is food, that no one will be without a roof over their head as long as there is shelter," he said.

In Papua New Guinea, a man's wealth is not judged by how much a person possesses, but often by how much he has given away. In the

highlands for example one of the most obvious demonstrations of the concept is the Moka ceremony during which members of individual villages pool their resources and give away vast wealth to neighbouring villages every three years or so. Their status is determined by how much they give away, with many borrowing well beyond their means to gain their kudos.

Though Sam is not from the Highlands, he recounted similar rituals within his own community.

"It encourages understanding and creates a sense of bonding and reliance," he says.

"By borrowing from one another to provide a gift, new friendships and alliances are made."

The more we talk about traditional life and Sam's village the more he questions his own role in Port Moresby.

"This country's law and order problem is getting more and more out of hand and I am concerned for my village," he says.

"The Minister wants me in Port Moresby because that's where he feels I can be of most help but I'm not so sure."

"But what about the comforts you have there – government housing and allowances, an office, a car, people working for you..........?" I ask.

"I don't need any of that. I am not really an office person. I don't know how to handle these meetings and do all that paper work. In my village I know exactly what I am and what I have to do and my people know as well. In Port Moresby it's just confusing. It's difficult to know who to trust or even see what is being achieved."

In two weeks Sam and I covered many subjects, as many about my country and culture as his. We talked about everything from tribal fighting to feminism, sorcery to single life and, as a result of our time together, I think we have forged a good friendship.

As expatriates, it is unrealistic to think we can learn about the traditional values of Papua New Guinea from the country's urban centres or hope to understand it without time and guidance from the people who have been raised by those values. In two weeks I have been given a brief insight into the values and priorities of the Wampur people and have some idea what it must have been like before outside influences started to change their value system.

As many before me have noted, it is disheartening to see the confusion and damage that is taking place as one dominating culture exerts its influence over another. Change is inevitable and much is likely to be lost and gained in the process.

If nothing else, our trip has made me realise that it is the responsibility of both cultures to try and understand and preserve the best of what the other has to offer. For Sam, who has experienced both cultures, a difficult decision lies ahead as he will soon have to decide whether he can do more for his country than for his village.

Whatever the outcome, I wish him every success and by this story thank him for the insight he provided.

Footnote: It is now three weeks after we returned. Sam has since handed in his resignation and declined an offer of promotion to return to his village.

Opposite page: The people of the Wampur village put on a special performance for Sam and me. There were no bright colours or theatrical props, though by the audience's reaction, it could have been a command performance.

VILLAGE SORCERY

CHAT WITH THE SPIRIT WORLD
– EXORCISING A BUAI HUSK AND TWO DWARFS
TEETH FROM SAM'S STOMACH – MY TURN

I witnessed a performance of sorcery today. Although it wasn't quite your average Speilberg production, it offered an interesting insight into village life in Papua New Guinea.

We were at Sam's village in the Morobe Province. I'd shown an interest in meeting a sorcerer and was introduced to a blond haired man who, if nothing else, certainly demonstrated an aloofness that accorded him a particular status among the group that surrounded us. I was told he was the youngest of several sorcerers in the region. In his presence Sam told me about some of the sorcery he had performed. Mysterious illnesses miraculously cured; arrows shot into the air that turned the sky to thunderclouds and lightning before returning to the hands of the sorcerer; visions of the future that had unfolded as predicted.

Our conversation made me curious to witness a demonstration of sorcery and both Sam and the sorcerer were obliging. "Let's drive out of the village a short way so people can't see us," said Sam, pointing out that it was a precaution that ensured the neighbouring clan could not accuse the sorcerer of casting a spell on them.

The demonstration began when the sorcerer squatted and pulled out two pale white conch shells, balancing one upon the other in an effort to make contact with the spirit world. He rotated the top shell, spat ginger into the air and muttered under his breath until contact was made. Then, using the shells as a telephone to the spirit world he held one to his ear and spoke into the other. Whispered Sam: "I have been sick for some time and the sorcerer is planning to cure me. He says it is something in my stomach but we don't know what it is so he's asking the spirits."

With that the sorcerer rose. He had put the shells down and was holding the stalk of a young banana tree in his hand. Shaving the ends off, he started spitting ginger on each end, again muttering incantations. Then he held it to Sam's stomach and begin twisting it.

"I can feel heat and something pulling inside my stomach as he moves it around," said Sam. At different intervals the sorcerer spat ginger onto his stomach and wiped it across his face, then he stood up and bit into the stalk, mauling it like a corn cob. Sam watched intently, as did his son who was watching the sorcerer perform for the first time.

Suddenly the sorcerer spat something onto the ground – a dark, round shape. Sam picked it up; a betelnut husk wrapped in copper wire.

"I knew it," burst Sam.

"This has been in my stomach for about a month. I recognise the Betelnut husk."

I was confused and Sam explained. "The person who poisoned me followed me until I threw away the betelnut and then collected it and took it to another sorcerer to poison me. I know who it was. The person was jealous of my job," said Sam.

Next to us the sorcerer was still mauling the banana stalk. Two more objects were spat onto the ground – two teeth.

"Dwarf's teeth, a further sign of the poisoning," said Sam with conviction. The sorcerer stood back triumphant; the consultation over.

Sam was visibly elated at the sorcerer's findings and said he felt a lot

Top Left: Sam stood relieved, the ginger and lime still drying on his chest." The Beletnut shell wrapped in wire and the two dwarf's teeth have been taken from my stomach. I feel much better," he said.

Above: The sorcerer demonstrated an aloofness and self–confidence that set him aside from the other people in the village. Sorcery still plays an important part in village life where many people do not understand or can afford the benefits of modern medicine.

Left: Sam picked the objects up as the sorcerer spat them onto the ground. "They were put inside me by another sorcerer and someone who wanted to see me dead."

better. It was a simple demonstration of the sorcerer's powers said Sam but obviously one that left little doubt in his mind about his powers.

Well, I must say, it all had me curious and I asked Sam if the sorcerer would mind giving me a quick check. It was an unusual request but the sorcerer said he'd see what he could do and reached into his bag for the shells. I took my shirt off and the ginger was chewed and spat across my body as the muttering again started in earnest. Five minutes later he arrived at his diagnosis.......... there was nothing wrong with me.

And he was right.

COMPENSATION

KINA AND PIGS – HIJACKED – DRAGGED THROUGH THE STREETS – ASARO MUDMEN PAY UP

The fact that Sam's complexion had turned sheet white (no mean feat for a Melanesian) was a clear indication there was reason for concern. About 30 armed warriors had leapt into the back of our rented utility, demanding to be taken to where the opposition clan was waiting to settle a compensation dispute.

It was only about half an hour earlier we had driven into the Eastern Highlands capital of Goroka on the second stage of our tour through the Morobe and Highlands regions. Our visit to Lae, about 100 kms to the east, had been cut short by a political upheaval that threatened to topple the provincial government. The fact the town had been completely boarded up, arms were being secretly circulated and riot police had been flown in from neighbouring provinces to deal with the situation, gave considerable speed to our premature departure.

So into Goroka we drove to be halted by a procession of about one hundred people on foot moving out of the town. Nearly everyone – men, women and children – had their faces painted in coloured mud – a sign, according to Sam, that they meant business and anticipated violence. They were singing and screaming as they passed, bows strained in mock demonstration of what was to come.

An onlooker told us two young men of the Watabung tribe had been killed in a car accident a week earlier by a drunken member of the Asaro (the mudmen) clan. Four thousand kina and several big pigs had been demanded as compensation for the loss and they were off to collect.

Understandably, Sam wasn't eager to follow the procession but with the assurance that I would trail at a safe distance, he agreed to come along. After about 10 minutes, and learning we had another three kilometres to go before reaching the opposing clan, I asked Sam to take the wheel so I could take some pictures. Reluctantly he agreed.

So, the car pulled over and Sam jumped into the driver's seat. I got out, walked around and jumped into the passenger's seat. About 20 warriors appeared from the bushes and jumped into the back of the ute. Not good. Sam was sitting there blubbering in language as machetes were slapped against the roof with everyone screaming for us to take them to the battle (yeah right guys!).

The alternatives looked grim. Men blocked the doorways, discounting our most immediate intention of bolting for the bushes, nor could we just accelerate out of it as we'd likely flatten half the procession (and God knows the compensation we'd have to pay). So we had no alternative but to take them to where they wanted to go....."Right Sam?"

Silence.

So there we were pottering along in the middle of the procession of screaming warriors armed to the teeth and ready for battle.

"If only the Justice Minister could see us now," I said to Sam in a bid for levity.

".........The national law and order delegation carting a truck load of warriors to a compensation battle. And what about the hire car company. If they had any idea of what we were doing with this car. Imagine the bloody premium!!"

Still silence.

As we came within about 100 metres of where the opposing clan was

Opposite Page: Word had long filtered back that the Asaro clan had been gathering the compensation payment for the Watabung tribe, so the likelihood of a battle had diminished considerably. Still, it seemed strange to see a baby's face in the middle of a crowd intent on demonstrating its willingness to fight if its demands were not met.

Above: The compensation procession skirted the centre of Goroka and progressed for several kilometres to where the offending tribe was waiting. The grieving next of kin were travelling in front and on foot, some carrying bows and axes. A convoy of supporters in cars and trucks followed close behind.

Above Right: To demonstrate the extent of their loss, women cover their faces in mud and scream hysterically. Others shave their heads or rip out clumps of their own hair to show their grief.

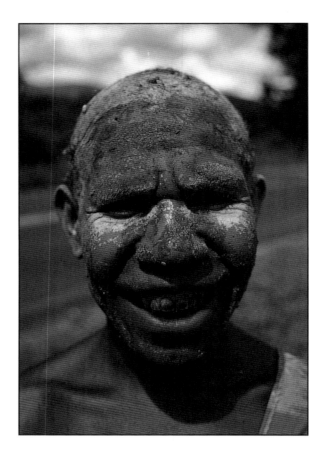

said to be waiting, the procession came to a halt and regrouped. Those in the back of our car alighted, many reaching inside our cabin to shake our hands and thank us for the lift.

Suddenly the wall of people cleared and a frail old woman appeared at the window to shake my hand. It was her sons that had been killed a week earlier. Feeling less threatened and that I should pay her the appropriate respect I got out of the car and shook her hand. The crowd gathered around in appreciation of the gesture, shuffling me away from the car. The next thing I knew, we were wandering in the direction of the opposing clan, her leathery hands clasping firmly onto mine. I'm suggesting it was not my place to be here but she was looking up at me with a toothless grin as if I was some sort of honoured guest. Breaking loose of some little old lady wasn't the concern. Facing the army that followed, however, was.

Over the crowd, I could see Sam trailing behind in the car as if to say you got yourself into this........

About 100 members of the Asaro tribe had gathered around a thin trunk of bamboo which towered high into the sky. Pinned to its length were thousands of Kina notes and at its base lay several large pigs, the compensation payment demanded by the Watabung people.

There was further chanting as the armed warriors ran around the Asaro leaders flaunting their strength and status. Speeches were made from both sides about the loss, the great tribute and the prevented bloodshed.........some of which I'm happy to say was mine.

Left: I got out of the car to pay the appropriate respect to the mother of the two deceased men (pictured) and found myself at the head of the procession being led towards the opposing tribe.

HIRI MOALE

THE ORIGINS OF THE HIRI VOYAGE – ARRIVAL OF THE LAKATOI – THE FESTIVAL – THE FINALE

Motuan legend has it the Hiri or trade voyage of the Motu people to the Gulf of Papua began in the early eighteenth century when food supplies had dwindled along the coastal reaches of the Central Province. Yam harvests had failed and inhabitants were dying from starvation and disease.

Enter the hero of the Hiri tale, Edai Boera, a fisherman who was cruising around nearby Hidiha Island when "Divara", the eel spirit, grabbed hold of him and pulled him to the depths.(You skeptics may laugh but a few of his mates saw the whole thing, dived down to help, and found Edai's feet poking out of a rock wall looking like Arthur's Excalibur.)

It was during his underwater sojourn Edai was schooled in the art of making a Lakatoi – a large ocean going vessel capable of sailing great distances. The eel spirit told him the great vessel was the answer to all his people's problems.

Confident the eel hadn't spun him a curly one, Edai returned to share his experience with his village and, although the initial response was not encouraging ("Yeah right Edai, tell us another one"), hunger soon persuaded everyone to give the idea a try and they set about building the Lakatoi.

They began by carving two large canoes then lashed them together into a single vessel, eventually adding a platform, a huge shelter, two masts and a set of claw like sails.

Impressed by the scale of his vision, the villagers grew more confident with Edai's idea and were soon loading the Lakatoi with ornaments and clay pots – specialities of the area – and heading off at wind speed in the general direction of the Gulf. Several months later when the south easterly trade winds turned north westerly the Lakatoi returned crammed with treasures of sago, betel-nut and timber. A period of feasting and celebration followed, Edai set up a business as a Lakatoi consultant and eventually retired on a cultural aid grant. To this day the Hiri (at least in part) is still the most celebrated event of the Motu calendar.

The 1950's saw the last of the authentic Hiri journeys (It seemed a bit crazy to spend three months at sea for a meal of Sago when you could buy tinned fish at the local store) but today part of the great journey is re-enacted to coincide with the country's September 16th Independence celebrations and the Hiri Moale Festival.

The more public side of the three day festivities begins on Saturday morning when the Lakatoi arrives at Ela Beach (ignore the weekend's calendar of events which says it all starts at 9am. In several decades of progress, punctuality is one thing that hasn't changed). By midday the giant crab claw sails are making an appearance on the horizon, flailing around in the strong sea breeze like they've been dropped in a pot. Slowly (painstakingly) the Lakatoi makes its way from nearby Local Island – pulled, pushed, and guided by a fleet of small power boats struggling in the absence of divine intervention. (Traditionally, two holy men or "Doritauna" were confined in the hull of the vessel in constant communion with the spirits to ensure a safe and speedy voyage).

Having spent three hours on the beach in the blazing sun, the waiting crowd is just as anxious as the ceremony's ancestors for the vessel's arrival. Old women are howling in celebration and slapping wood against

Opposite Page: Huge claw-like sails characterise the Lakatoi. Construction of the vessel begins weeks in advance of the Hiri Moale festival, with responsibility rotated among the villages along the coast. The twin hull of the Lakatoi is generally built on the mainland and then transported to Local Island, off Ela Beach. The men of the village live on the island until the huge vessel is completed.

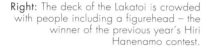

Right: The deck of the Lakatoi is crowded with people including a figurehead – the winner of the previous year's Hiri Hanenamo contest.

pieces of tin while hundreds scuttle down to the waterline to witness the arrival. Soon the Lakatoi is clearly in sight, clamouring with men and a single bare breasted woman – the figurehead – holding her arms aloft with grass skirt swaying. As the crowd on the beach surges forward, so too does the Lakatoi, crashing through protective pylons and ungraciously beaching itself with a jar that threatened to abandon its cargo. (The figurehead would have done well to hang on). The crowd is delighted, the band bursts into tune and the speeches start.

All up, it's a great day. Apart from the arrival of the Lakatoi, scores of people from Motuan villages parade in their traditional finery and the first heat of the Miss Hiri Hanenamo Quest is held.

Day two of the Hiri Moale Festival is pretty ho–hum, unless you're into local sport, sailing or Church services. It's a good time to just walk around as, like Christmas day, everyone you see radiates a feeling of goodwill.

The final day culminates at the Hubert Murray Stadium (just follow the traffic) where thousands of people cram into the grounds to see the traditional dancing, the car floats and the crowning of the Miss Hiri Hanenamo. It's a spectacular gathering of colour and finery, with police bands, traditional dancing, singing and drama.

At about three o'clock a procession of bare breasted girls files onto the grounds with their arms aloft, hypnotising an appreciative crowd with their swaying grass skirts. Though a new addition to the festivities of the Hiri Moale, they are easily (and understandably methinks) the most popular attraction. Old men and women – the guardians of traditional custom – scrutinise each contestant, studying their tattoos, their ornamentation and their movements. Out of more than 20 contestants, one Miss Hiri Hanenamo is named and the crowd roars its delight, the culmination of a spectacular three day celebration of traditional Motu custom.

Above: Pristine beaches typify the coastline of the Central Province, from where the famous Hiri Moale ceremony originated.

BEAUTY CONTEST
THE QUEST FOR MISS HIRI HANENAMO

Curious about what it takes to win the Miss Hiri Hanenamo contest?

This year 23 young Hanenamo hopefuls vied for the coveted Motu title with five judges rating each contestant out of a potential score of 100.

The contest began on Port Moresby's Ela Beach with the arrival of the Lakatoi. Contestants paraded in front of the judges and were graded from 1 to 20 for their poise, deportment and dancing abilities. Special consideration was also given to their confidence and the way they responded to their first public appearance. Then it was off to a nearby venue where the serious scrutiny began. Out of 60 points, up to 20 were offered for the costumes, 20 for their tattoos and another 20 for their knowledge of the Hiri journey and Motu custom. The final points were based on crowd popularity during a parade at Hubert Murray Stadium.

In the costume section points are deducted for deviating from tradition and using items such as pieces of plastic and coloured tinsel. Additional points, however, are given to those demonstrating more subtle dress codes such as the use of a knotted piece of string, traditionally kept in the house of the Baditauna (spiritual leader) by his daughters or mother to indicate how many days he had been at sea on the Lakatoi.

As is obvious by the contestants, body tattoos play a major part in the quest for Miss Hiri Hanenamo. The girls are judged not just for the use of them but also on their knowledge of their design's significance. Although indelible felt pen appears to have replaced more permanent methods, generally each of the contestants has a small permanent tattoo somewhere on their body.

There is a range of different tattoos, each one with a particular significance. The tear drop tattoo just beneath the eye signifies the first born girl of a Lakatoi captain; the tattoo on the lower leg is worn by any woman whose father journeyed on the Lakatoi, and the wishbone design over the collarbone signifies payment of bride price.

The third part of the quest – the question and answers section –is often considered the most difficult by the contestants who are expected to be thoroughly versed on Motu tradition. In 1971 when the contest was first held, few of the contestants had the faintest idea what their tattoos represented or knew about different aspects of the Hiri festival. Today, however, word has spread about what the judges are expecting and crash courses in Hiri history are undertaken prior to the contest. Who was the hero of the Lakatoi legend? What was the Lakatoi's cargo? etc, all asked in Motu rather than Pidgin or English. You get zero points for what used to be the typical response of "Mum gave it to me" when asked where the toea armshells came from or how the grass skirts are made.

Day three of the Hiri Moale Festival is the big one. The contestants in a final parade are judged for the last 20 points. As I discovered, the western concept of beauty has little place in the contest. By my score card the girl with the beaming smile and the fine curves was destined to win hands down, however, she was eclipsed by a larger girl with the more pendulous movements ....a decision which obviously left the parents of the other contestants similarly unconvinced.

Opposite page: The contestants exhibit a beauty made more captivating by their girlish innocence and charm.

Above & Right: Two future contenders for the Hiri Hanenamo title.

Opposite page: Winner of the Hiri Hanenamo Beauty Contest. The beauty contest is a recent addition to the Hiri Moale festivities and the competition is fierce as women vie for the coveted Motu title which will bring honour to their village. The contest culminates in a dance parade before a huge crowd at Hubert Murray Stadium.

RASCALS

THEIR ORIGINS – WHY THEY COMMIT CRIME – PORT MORESBY UNDER SIEGE – – POLICE RESPONSE – THE FUTURE

The rascal problem throughout Papua New Guinea dominates the news and thoughts of many people in this country. Reference to crimes committed is a daily occurrence – their frequency, their brutality and their vicinity.

Dr Bruce Harris titles his 50 page discussion paper "The Rise of Rascalism". After several years studying criminal social trends in America and Jamaica, he arrived in Papua New Guinea and spent two years at snooker tables and beer halls involved in what he calls "face to face research with the rascals and their gangs." He completed the report in March, 1988.

The following is a summary of his findings.

Dr Harris introduces his report by questioning past methods to combat the increasing level of lawlessness in PNG. "If we were forming a policy on the medical profession, we would talk to doctors and nurses. If we were making a policy in the legal field we would talk to lawyers and judges. Yet for several decades we have formulated and implemented programmes to deal with law and order without taking the time to talk to people involved in the criminal activity. Everyone has a solution to the problem of rascal gangs but no one understands what the problem really is."

According to Dr Harris, rascal gangs originated in Port Moresby in the early 1960's as loose groups of disillusioned youths, usually immigrants from outlying areas, bonded together by common circumstances. They arrived with high expectations of wealth and modern living but abruptly discovered both were in short supply.

Traditional village life and particularly the "Wantok" system did little to prepare them for what they found. The idea that one could suffer in the midst of plenty contradicted the individual's most basic traditional beliefs and values. In the village no one person went hungry as long as the community had food. As they quickly discovered, in the cities it was all different. Suddenly, they were left to fend for themselves.

For the young it was both perplexing and frustrating that there could be people with such immense wealth living alongside so many who had so little. Even more confusing was that there was a law that condoned the selfishness of the rich and appeared to prevent the poor from sharing in their good fortune. The only way out was to work, but opportunities were scarce. As their circumstances became worse they started to resent the system they believed was responsible for their circumstances.

It was this social climate that gave birth to the rascal gangs.

Dr Harris identifies the lifting of prohibition in 1962 as one of the primary causes for the accelerated growth of rascal gangs. Drinking alcohol became a rite of passage for young men wishing to show they were "modernised". By 1970 domestic beer production had multiplied by eight times its 1964 figure, imported beer sales had doubled and Port Moresby alone had more than 100 outlets. With beer readily identified as a symbol of social status, associated crime increased – either direct theft of alcohol or theft of goods which were exchanged for alcohol.

Dr Harris says the rascal gangs in Port Moresby underwent considerable change between 1960 and the present day. From bands of rebellious

Above: Dr Bruce Harris (pictured) produced an insightful study on the rascal gangs of Papua New Guinea and discovered many similarities with other countries in the world. As he points out, the symptoms of the problem are all too familiar, but what should be different - particularly based on the failure of other countries to successfully combat crime - are the ways authorities are currently seeking to address the problems.

youths, they evolved into organised gangs – The Texas Gang, Raipex, Joes Mob, Laddies, The Mafia and KKK. Gang clashes in the early 1970's were common as small groups were absorbed into those more powerful.

It wasn't long before the rascals realised co-operation was more profitable than competition. By this stage they had merged into about a dozen primary gangs. In response to the escalating crime, police launched "sweeps" or raids to confiscate stolen goods and arrest offenders. But according to Dr Harris the tactic was ineffective and only served to alienate the general community. All valuable goods without receipts were liable for confiscation and those in possession were likely to be arrested. The police sweeps also encouraged the development of tighter gang organisation and greater secrecy. Dr Harris argues the police would have been better to seek the co-operation of the community by enlisting the assistance of village elders.

By the late 70's the gangs had become more organised. Educated youths – taught enough to want, but not enough to get it – started running with the packs. Many eventually led them. The rascal gang's methods became more sophisticated, break and enters were better planned and distribution of stolen goods was more efficient. A siege mentality swept Port Moresby. Houses were soon surrounded by barbed wire fences and iron bars were built into windows.

Ironically, Police statistics did little to reflect the enormity of the problem, in fact they indicated crime was on the decrease. Dr Harris refers to an authoritative law and order report commissioned during the period:

"This declining crime trend poses a perplexing riddle: how can statistics show crime is declining when everyone's experience suggests an exploding increase. Sadly the solution to this riddle is very simple. Police statistics are abysmally wrong!"

By the mid-1980's only five percent of stolen goods was being recovered. Seven percent of stolen vehicles and three percent of break and enters resulted in arrest. The situation was out of control. In 1985, a state of emergency was declared. Little has improved since.

According to Dr Harris, rascal gangs of the future will evolve along three distinct paths. They will become more organised, developing highly efficient distribution networks for stolen goods both in national and overseas markets. As profits increase, so too will the gangs ability to recruit new members. The number of so-called victimless crimes – extortion and drugs – will sky-rocket. Internally people will pay protection money to the gangs and incredibly powerful drug syndicates will develop, influencing all levels of the community.

Dr Harris says rascals will work with politicians and businessmen in their mutual interests. Both parties will use the rascals to exact "payouts" from their opposition or hinder the operations of their business rivals. He says it is already happening but, as with most of the operations rascals are involved in, it will become far more organised and widespread.

And so ends Dr Harris's report, commissioned by the Institute of Applied Social and Economic Research. Apparently its release sparked considerable controversy, mainly generated by politicians fearing implication.

PMV'S

GETTING AROUND IN THE NATIONAL CAPITAL
ROAD WARRIORS – BEST SERVICE IN THE WORLD
PUNISHMENT OR PROFIT – THE CHALLENGE

There are few things on Port Moresby roads more intimidating than the sight in your rear vision mirror of a PMV bearing down on you at time warp velocity with a buai chomping Chimbu at the wheel.

Few who have braved the major arteries of the national capital would not have experienced the trauma.

Public Motor Vehicles (commonly called PMV's) are to Port Moresby what buses are anywhere else in the world, only they are about half the size and seat about 30 people. According to the Department of Transport's Motor Registry Office, there are 477 of them currently registered in the National Capital District. Ask most car drivers, and that's 477 vehicles that have just screeched from the set of The Road Warrior or Death Race 2000.

Characteristic of the capital's carriers is their erratic manoeuvring, the breakneck speeds at which they travel and their unpredictability. A steady flow of traffic can come to a sudden halt while one driver – deliberately oblivious to the congestion – shares a yarn with his Wantok. And woe betide you if you're travelling in the left lane and a PMV driver travelling on your right sees a potential fare to your left. There are the random reversals, the blaring horns and the squid–like diversion of exhaust fumes, the glaring looks, the abusive tirades and the buai, all waiting to be heaped on you from a great height at the slightest provocation.

According to the PMV Drivers Association which was established in 1981 to represent the interests of the PMV drivers, Port Moresby has one of the cheapest and most efficient public transport systems in the world. Says Association spokesman Emmanuel Rausi, "The average waiting time for a PMV is just four minutes and the maximum cost to travel any route is only 40 Toea."

Mr Rausi says that contrary to belief, there has been a marked decrease in the number of PMVs in Port Moresby over recent years due to increased competition, which he concedes could be responsible for "the sometimes reckless nature of the drivers."

Although the maximum fare is 40 Toea, drivers are undercutting each other and passengers are paying 25–30 toea a ride. That means drivers are having to drive twice as far (fast?) to make a living. On an average, the PMV driver works up to 12 hours a day, six days a week and can look to earn about K150 a fortnight. That's allowing for the free travel of Wantoks and those who get off the PMV and refuse to pay.

According to Mr Rausi, PMV drivers used to be mainly from the Morobe Province, however, today they are predominantly Highlanders. Fifty one percent of them are owner operators. He says many Highlanders have cashed in their coffee crops to move down to Port Moresby, attracted by the apparent ease of making money by driving a PMV.

Mr Rausi says his association is aware that there is a problem with speeding but adds that for every person who complains about the speed, there is someone else who is grateful for it.

"We try and educate our drivers to slow down – especially the young ones – but the policing of traffic is slack and drivers know that nobody will stop them for speeding or driving recklessly. The Association also has a growing concern about the number of second hand PMV's on the roads,

Above: A PMV driver in one of his friendlier moments. The last one I saw had his PMV up on two wheels as he overtook me. Indelibly etched in my mind is the fanatic grin of the driver arched over the steering wheel and roaring defiance as he passed.

Below: Cartoonist Bob Browne's version of a local PMV.

LAISENS TO KILL..
CLASS 6.. ISSUE TO ALL PMV DRIVERS AFTER COMPLETING BASIC RAMBO TRAINING COURSE

particularly those being bought from government departments. The average life of a PMV is three years but buses are being bought second hand and repaired for public transport without proper regard for safety. Our association is taking a responsible approach and is trying to work with the Department of Transport and Police to educate drivers and enforce safety laws," he said.

Personally, I have had only a few run-ins with PMV drivers. I was once deliberately parked in for 10 minutes while a PMV disgorged its human cargo. Incensed by the purpose with which he pulled up, I got out of my car, took one look at the driver responsible for my predicament and mustered the courage to do little more than mutter under my breath. On another occasion I found myself racing a PMV. It was in my earlier days in Port Moresby when I had the good fortune to be driving a sports car. I was driving home from work when I pulled up at the lights alongside a PMV and looked out and up to catch the eye of its driver. Suddenly it's all on. He was revving his engine and spitting buai with excitement while his co–pilot was hard against the windscreen anxiously anticipating the green light.

I should probably add at this point that I had never owned a sports car before, in fact the closest I have come to real speed was in the days of my schooling when, without permission, I borrowed and crashed my parent's brand new vehicle. (Sadly, the speed I reached as a consequence was not enough to escape my father's lengthy stride). So it was understandable that with the slight depression of the accelerator that sent lights and needles whirring, I was hard pressed to suppress my urge to surge.

Through the din of the PMV's diesel engine alongside me, I could feel the confident purring of my car's motor and as the light turned green, I flattened it...... and watched the whining juggernaut disappear into the depths of my rear vision mirror.

Some time later, while casually cruising down Two Mile Hill, the PMV suddenly re–appeared two inches from my bumper bar, weaving from left to right with horn blaring, passengers screaming and lights flashing. It was apparent the race was not over. Persistent I thought, but no problem, and once again accelerated down the winding road. I was fairly well flying around a bend when this PMV up on two bloody wheels passed me. Indelibly etched in my mind was the fanatic grin of the driver, arched over the steering wheel and roaring defiance. At the rear window of the PMV the 20 or so passengers – once screaming in excitement – were shrieking in terror, their distorted expressions pressed hard against the glass.

So I decided to abandon my bid for glory and returned to the sedentary pace of the rest of the traffic, eventually arriving at the base of the hill where the driver and co-pilot – in a PMV surrounded by people trampled in the exodus of passengers – waved me on with laughter.

Right: A born-again Christian recently granted citizenship, cartoonist Bob Browne (pictured) has spent years trying to understand the people of PNG. "The Melanesian sense of humour is not necessarily a highly intellectual one but it's by no means inferior – just different. The ranking of intellectual humour in western societies can be very high, whereas here it is nowhere near as important."

GRASS ROOTS

THE MAN BEHIND THE CARTOON –
WHAT TICKLES PNG'S FUNNY BONE –
SOMETHING SERIOUS TO LAUGH ABOUT

It has been more than 10 years since Grass Roots – Papua New Guinea's most popular cartoon character – made it known he wanted to be the Prime minister of the country. Since then he's hardly been out of the press.

In one of his recent antics, Grass (alias "Rambo Roots") waged a military offensive on PNG's public service by hitting at the heart of government operations and attempting to cut off its buai supplies. In another headline seeking effort, he wrote to Queen Elizabeth demanding a knighthood and threatened to send over his wantoks (relatives) to live in her palace for six months if it wasn't immediately forthcoming. He reckons tribal fighting is just a highlander's answer to unemployment; says the French in the Pacific should export Tahitian women not atomic bombs; and regularly accuses all politicians and businessmen of being crooks ("Them assfiring politisins and bisnismen").

Grass, though he's unlikely to admit it, isn't your average comic book hero. He runs a black market beer outlet at Six Mile in Port Moresby and spends most of the day chewing buai and trying to come up with new get–rich–quick schemes. In a vulnerable moment he admits to being a lazy, unemployed slob who bludges off his wantoks, gets drunk and fights with his wife.

Whatever his shortfalls, Grass's popularity among both nationals and expatriates in PNG is undisputed. Three times a week his comments are guaranteed space in the country's highest circulating newspaper. His picture also features on wall calendars in offices and homes around the nation and he's the star of a prolific greeting card business. "There's a bit of Grass in all of us," echoes an army of loyal supporters.

Bob Browne, the creator of the Grass Roots character, says he is continually amazed by the cartoon's popularity among both nationals and expatriates. He attributes much of it to the fact that Grass identifies well with his namesake – the grass roots people of PNG.

"To me, Grass is the incorrigible rascal – in the western sense of the word – who everyone can relate to. He is a well meaning, good hearted, self seeking bludger."

"He's become a bit of a cultural hero in that he reflects much of what the grass root people think about in life. He's particularly interested in their life and – as is often the case – when people show interest in you, you become interested in them."

Bob Browne was 25 when he arrived in Papua New Guinea in 1971 as a volunteer worker from England. He had applied for a job as a printer with a Catholic mission in Wewak through a British recruitment agency after embellishing his resume to win the job.

It was not long after the plane touched down in PNG that Bob realised he had seriously landed himself in it. He took one look at the printing machine and didn't even know where to start. "....So what can you do?" queried a perplexed, though sympathetic, mission supervisor.

"Well", said Bob, "I'm not bad at design and I can take a pretty good photograph."

Bob spent two years at the Catholic mission before joining The Creative Arts Centre in Port Moresby (now the National Arts school) as

Right & Opposite page: An obvious gesture made in the middle of a public arena and a carving etched into the front of a police station offer a light-hearted look at some of the things that make the people of PNG laugh.

head of its graphics department. He returned briefly to England but couldn't settle – "It was the classic culture shock thing, everyone seemed to have such shallow values, no one had it together" – so he came back to Papua New Guinea and the Arts School in 1974.

At that stage, Bob's sketches were little more than doodles at the top of the page but in 1976 an opportunity arose to create a cartoon character for a local car company. It was the birth of Isuzu Lu, Bob's first commercial cartoon success story, soon to be followed by the character Grass Roots and Bob's own business, the Grass Roots Comic Company.

"Both Isuzu Lu and Grass filled a need among the people in PNG for someone to identify with, a home–grown character that was unique to the country," said Bob.

"People wanted to see something funny that wasn't coming down on dumb Kanakas". Before Grass Roots there were several publications, one in particular called 'Black and White', which was incredibly racist. Grass Roots came along at a time when people wanted to see something different and positive that highlighted the true character of the Melanesian people, something they could see in a page of newsprint and say that cartoon is distinctly Melanesian."

Bob says Grass looks to exploit the humorous differences between the western and Melanesian cultures by bringing two extremes together. "Clothing the essential Melanesian nature in the 1990's", as he puts it . As an example he talks of Grass Roots' black market liquor store – typically a ramshackle hut with wire windows – and combines it with Grass's vision of seeing it with electronic check–out systems and turnstiles.

According to Bob the people of Papua New Guinea love to laugh at themselves and like most people they're always looking for something to laugh at.

"The Melanesian sense of humour tends to be more slapstick and the success of a joke often depends more on the telling of the story than the punch–line," says Bob.

"Papua New Guineans are great orators and strong emphasis is placed on the use of language, innuendo and intonation." That's why you often see people laughing while the story is being told, rather than as it concludes.

"Because the country's population is so linguistically diverse and much of its people's traditional knowledge is handed down through the spoken rather than the written word, Papua New Guineans can be incredibly creative in their use of language. They delight on the simple play of words....... one that springs to mind for example is the use of the word 'Pig Pen', the adjective to describe someone who is dirty. Though relatively uninspiring on its own, local people may laugh at the suggestion that a pig has a pen (biro)."

Bob says there is still much about the Melanesian sense of humour he is yet to understand. He still, for the life of him, can't work out why, in the middle of a particularly touching scene at the movies, people are curling over with laughter.

"The Melanesian sense of humour is not necessarily a highly intellectual sense of humour but it is by no means inferior –just different. The ranking of intellectual humour in western societies can be very high, whereas in Papua New Guinea it is nowhere near as important," says Bob.

Asked if there are any areas he has avoided in his efforts to make Melanesians laugh, Bob says sex is the most obvious.

"The people of PNG have very high morals, and humour about sex is a dead loss. In contrast to Australians for example who tend to be very forward and frank, Melanesian people are shy and generally prefer to keep intimate aspects of their lives to themselves. They become embarrassed with intimacy and often giggle when they are uncomfortable. Sadly, however, that attitude is changing with the influence of western models."

Humour – as Bob is the first to admit – is a fickle medium as not everyone sees a joke the same way. There have been times when he's received hate mail calling him a colonialist and a bigot and, on one particular occasion, a clan of Hanuabadan's threatened to tear his office down because of one of his cartoons.

"I guess there have only been about four incidents in 10 years but generally, I'd like to think I'm pretty sensitive to my readership. I guess, like most cartoonists though, you have to be willing to take a chance sometimes."

In 1989 Bob Browne became a Papua New Guinean citizen, a decision which he admits has altered his perspective and may well add an element of seriousness to some of his work.

"Humour can be an effective medium for change and I think that now this is my home, I have a greater responsibility to attract people's attention to areas which are important to the interests of this country. There may be scope to develop as a political cartoonist. There are two issues I feel particularly strongly about – the quality of leadership and a need for accountability. Both are areas no one appears willing to talk about and maybe humour is a good way to get the ball rolling."

So in 1990, as Grass celebrates the passing of his first decade in the public eye, Bob looks back on the past 10 years satisfied that he has brought laughter to the faces of thousands.

...........while, down at Six Mile, amid the clinking of black market beer bottles, Grass is about to despatch an urgent fax to "Misis Kwin" demanding to know why his name still hasn't been included in the New Year's honours list.

CRIME

CLOSE TO HOME

Port Moresby's crime situation inched closer to home this week with several incidents happening around me.

The week began with the stabbing of a priest outside Boroko's Green Jade Restaurant – in the same block as my office. The priest and three other men were leaving the restaurant when a group of youths assaulted them with knives and demanded their wallets. The concern was that the youths stabbed first and demanded later.

Wednesday lunchtime, just down from the restaurant, a man had his car broken into while he was returning with the staff payroll. Said someone from the crowd after the thieves had taken off "It was planned. They just pulled up in a car, lifted the lock from the outside of the car window and took the bag of money. Everyone just stood there and watched."

Four days later – Sunday – and I thought I'd drop into the office. The iron gate at the end of the arcade had been bent and a shop window was smashed inside. The locksmith, arriving early that morning, was working in his shop when he heard a window being smashed at the end of the arcade. He pulled out his .22 rifle and went to investigate, catching two rascals red handed. "There were four of them, all about 20 years old," he said. The two outside took off when he threatened to shoot the other two if they moved. "I don't know if I really would have shot them. I was so bloody scared. There could be payback involved, I'll have to be careful. But what could you do?"

Finally that afternoon, I was recounting the story to friends in my apartment block. That same week one of their friends living in Waigani was assaulted as she waited for her electronic gate to open. It was around sunset, her child was in the passenger seat. Suddenly the car door flew open and a man punched her in the face, knocking her cold. When she woke up her child was screaming and her purse and belongings were gone. "We saw her yesterday she looks terrible. She hasn't had a good nights sleep since it happened and her child keeps waking up screaming. Like so many other women, she just wants to go finish."

As a result, my neighbours have decided to hire a daytime guard.

Few expatriates I have met are not talking about the recent spate of crimes. Curfews are being self imposed, there are people purchasing personal firearms, and wives and families are being sent to live in Cairns while husbands commute to Port Moresby.

The situation here is growing worse. It's one thing reading about how bad the lawlessness is in Lae and the way it is deteriorating in Mt Hagen but it's not until things start happening closer to home that you really begin to realise just how dangerous it has all become.

BUSTED

BREAKING THE LAW – POLICE APPREHENSION
GAOL THREAT – JUST PUNISHMENT

I was pulled over by the police yesterday. It was bound to happen. Even in my most sedate moods I tend to drive like a maniac.

I took a wrong turn and corrected in obvious contradiction to the road rules.

In the passenger seat of the pursuing police car a young constable with clipboard wedged to the windscreen was eagerly copying my licence plate at the instruction of the senior officer beside him. Both were teetered on Hollywood pursuit mode, willing me to attempt a getaway.

After following me for two blocks (and having attracted the attention of a royal tour), Starsky and Hutch – with sirens wailing – decided to pull me over. As with anything slightly out of the ordinary, a crowd quickly gathered.

Of course at my first opportunity I responded with cries of innocence (as I have been known to do in the past, I would have cried tears if I thought it would spare me the fine) and mentioned my recent meeting with the Police Minister "......of course I did mention he's a personal friend of mine". But it fell on deaf ears. I was told I had turned illegally in a manner that was dangerous to the public. Quite obviously I was in the wrong and I was politely told that if my error had caused an accident I would have been thrown in gaol. A murmur of excitement rippled through the crowd.

By this stage the young constable had sensed my vulnerability and asked me for my licence.........which I had left at home.

"In PNG that's a fineable offence – that's two," said the senior officer. The young constable was barely able to contain his glee.

His boss continued.

"However........," he said, pausing thoughtfully.

"I have discretionary powers and believe you may have been unaware of the road rules or the need to carry your licence, so I ask only one thing..."

"Anything," I assured him.

"...... That you bring your licence into me personally at Boroko Police Headquarters tomorrow."

"But I have meetings all day and ......"

"By 11am," he reiterated, shaking my hand, parting the sea of spectators and trailing a speechless constable back to the car.

As expected, the next day I was flat out. I couldn't even remember his name. There's no way he'll remember who I am and this is PNG. He's hardly likely to track me down I reasoned.

But still, I decided to drop in anyway.

Arriving at the front desk of the station, he was visibly delighted and obviously surprised to see me. After composing himself, leading me to his office and taking down the details of my licence with painstaking formality ("I'm sorry to do this David but it is police procedure"), he called in his young constable.

"You see there is mutual respect between the police and the public," he boomed with pride.

"It doesn't matter whether you're black or white, the same laws apply."

He even called in two other officers who, with luck, are out there today waiting to try the same thing on someone else.

LAISENS
(LICENCE)

LITTLE PLASTIC CARD WITH 'ORRIBLE SNAPSHOT OF YOUR FACE.. FOR GETTING THROUGH POLIS ROD-BLOKS AN' GETTING INNOCENT SHOPKEEPERS TO ACCEPT YOUR CHEQUE

(NOT TO BE CONFUSE WITH ABILITY TO DRIVE A VEHICLE)

STOP POLICE

AVE 1

Above: Cartoonist Bob Browne looks at the lighter side of the law.

TOK PISIN

LEARNING PIDGIN – BLACKBIRDING
IS THERE A NEED TO LEARN – MAKING EXCUSES
YUMI MAS LAINIM TOK PISIN

Expatriate women be warned: standing on your front verandah and calling "Here puss puss" at the top of your lungs is likely to attract more men than cats.

Pus pus (pronounced puss puss) is Pidgin for sexual intercourse. One of the decisions many expatriates face when they arrive in Papua New Guinea is whether or not to learn Pidgin. The majority of expatriates in the country say it's unnecessary – particularly in urban centres – as English is Papua New Guinea's first language and there is rarely a need to speak Pidgin. Others argue that learning the language is an important part of assimilating the culture.

Pidgin, the country's second language, is spoken throughout Papua New Guinea. Authorities say it evolved in the late 19th century from the "blackbirding" days when more than 70,000 Pacific islanders were brought in to work the cane fields of Queensland. Pidgin was created from a melting pot of many different languages and returned to the Pacific islands with their people where it continued to develop under the influences of individual cultures. Today there are three distinct Pidgins spoken in the Pacific – Papua New Guinea Pidgin, Vanuatu Pidgin or Bislama, and Solomon Islands Pidgin.

In Port Moresby the main languages spoken are English, Pidgin and Motu, the language of the people of the Central Province in which the national capital is located. Having a third language to deal with can make practising Pidgin a dilemma, particularly in instances where you muster the courage to say the few words of Pidgin you know, only to have the recipient look at you in bewilderment because he only speaks Motu. Even worse (and I speak from experience) is when you don't know he's talking to you in Motu and think that what is being said is the Pidgin you thought you had already learnt!

Often the need to speak Pidgin depends on the work you are doing in Papua New Guinea and your attitude to the people. Unless you are working with Pidgin speaking nationals on a day–to–day basis, many expatriates see the only benefit of knowing the language is in a domestic situation, say with domestic help. Sign language is the common substitute for Pidgin, otherwise, most expatriates simply expect local people to speak to them in English.

Outside Port Moresby, Pidgin is more widely spoken, though the use of English is increasing. English is compulsory in schools (appreciating the cost to translate text books from English into Pidgin) and carries the status of the educated person's language. Bear in mind also that Papua New Guinea boasts more than 700 different languages, so it is likely most nationals you meet are at least bi–lingual.

According to Major Bruce Copeland, a defence force officer who has been teaching Papua New Guinea Pidgin for more than 13 years, there is still a great need for expatriates to learn Pidgin in PNG. He points out that while English may be the accepted language, Pidgin is the language in which most nationals prefer to converse. "It's the friendly language, the one nationals are more comfortable with in a social situation," he says.

"Many expatriates choose not to learn Pidgin because of the difficulties associated with learning a new language, yet it is relatively easy to learn

because it's so similar to English. It's only a matter of grasping the basic structures before you are comfortable enough to make your own progress," he says.

Major Copeland, who teaches Pidgin to personnel attached to the Australian High Commission in Port Moresby, says that as with any country, the people of Papua New Guinea appreciate the effort by expatriates to learn their language. It is a sign of respect and demonstrates a genuine desire to understand the culture. He says all too often, however, expatriates arrive here and make excuses for why they haven't bothered. "The fact that they don't speak the common language is a sad reflection of their inability to meet these people half way in their own country," he says.

Major Copeland is critical of those who claim Pidgin is a bastard language with little more than a few "yu save's" and "ims" added onto the verbs. He says it's no more a bastard language than English is to Latin.

"Pidgin is rich and colourful with distinct features that make it sound musical and often poetic. People say it is a limited language, not capable of expressing complex ideas. Do those people also believe that Papua New Guineans are incapable of complex thought? Rubbish! Anything I can understand I can express in Pidgin, whether it's political ideology, car mechanics or complex mathematics .... well, maybe not complex mathematics, but that's because I can't understand complex mathematics in bloody English!"

"To me English can be likened to a rich house full of luxury items. There is plenty to choose from, but most of what surrounds you, you can do without. Pidgin, on the other hand, is a simple and unpretentious house where you are comfortable and not surrounded by things you don't need. I often find myself preferring to speak Pidgin to nationals because I know exactly what I am saying and that it is being clearly understood."

Major Copeland says his method of teaching Pidgin is simple. It does not require an understanding of complex grammar and there is no need to slavishly memorize words.

"Pidgin is based on English – Pik (pig), dok (dog) Brata (brother), Haus (house) – and in my classes, people learn the language in parrot fashion. As children we are all great imitators until we begin to learn for ourselves and Pidgin is no different. It's just a matter of saying some key phrases over and over again until you are familiar with the basics. You just build on from there. People can understand Pidgin well before they speak it. I make a point of telling a couple of jokes to my class in Pidgin (he's renowned for them) and everyone laughs in the right places. They become more comfortable with a language they can understand. What other language offers that level of comprehension in the first day of instruction?"

He adds that Pidgin is also an entertaining language to learn, citing words such as "bugarup" for broken, "swit– biskit" for homosexual and "givem 60" for speeding.

All this talk of learning Pidgin may provoke you to wonder whether this author has yet mastered the local lingo. It needs to be said that my capacity for learning foreign languages would have seen me departing the Tower of Bable a mute. God knows, however, I've certainly tried to learn Pidgin. These past 12 months I have invested a fortune in Pidgin tapes, Pidgin books and at least one introductory Pidgin course (at the University)...all which have left me with little more than a "sori tu mas" or "tank yu tru."

But just as all seemed lost and I appeared destined never to include a foreign language to my resume, along came Bruce Copeland and his Pidgin classes. He promised that in just five days he would transform me from a five word weakling into a Pidgin speaking powerhouse. "Complete this 10 hour course", he said, "and you will graduate with "your 'P' plates to speaking Pidgin. In just five short lessons we'll have you understanding the language and drawing from a considerable vocabulary."

It all sounded too easy – instant Pidgin – but today, two weeks later, I can proudly report I have a reasonable and rapidly increasing grasp of the language. In hindsight the biggest hurdle I needed to overcome was the perception that learning Pidgin represented the trauma associated with learning a completely foreign language. The fact is, English equips you with much of the vocabulary before you even start.

Most importantly, however, having started using what I have learnt, it is clearly apparent that learning Pidgin really does make a difference – not just to the way you view PNG, but the way its people view you.

Left: The likelihood of running out of subjects to photograph in Papua New Guinea was slim. If your attention was not captivated by the spectacular landscapes or the activities, there were always the children.

CHEKI

NATIONAL LANDMARK – ROADSIDE SCAM – SUNDAY DRIVE – WATERING EYES – FAMILY PHOTO

On a good day "Cheki" earns as much as any PNG company executive. He is an entrepreneur with a keen sense of finance, a sound judgement of people and a tremendous flair for presentation – hence the bone in his nose.

Every Sunday he paints his face in the warlike colours of a highland warrior, dons his hat of human hair, ties a clump of "ass grass" to his waist and takes up bow and arrow to stand on a hill looking out from Varirata National Park, about 30 kms north of Port Moresby. There he waits in ambush to charge a steady stream of Sunday drivers two kina a pop to stand next to him and have their photographs taken.

It was the same year PNG gained independence, 1975, that Cheki took to the hills with his money making venture. Convinced that taking photographs was all expatriates came to his country to do (an impression based on his own observation) he dressed in traditional garb and stood where he knew everyone would see him.

It took him a while to muster the courage to start charging people to stand next to him. His initial fee was 20 Toea (25c) but with increased custom grew a confidence that has converted the eagerness of his audience into the tinkle of Kina coins.

Today Cheki is one of Port Moresby's most photographed landmarks, enjoying a reputation as exaggerated and colourful as the stories recounted by those who take his picture.

Inside the cars to Varirata it's your classic Sunday scene. The family stationwagon meandering up the winding mountain road. Dad's driving everyone round the bend because he won't play I–spy, Mum's threatening to make the three kids walk home if they don't stop their screaming and the family Labrador is in the back hanging his nose out of the window and farting with joy.

Amid the watering eyes and the wails of accusation, the car rounds the corner to see Cheki squatting above them with blood red Betel nut grin and bow and arrow poised. Ma shrieks, protectively swats the kids to a distant corner of the car and lunges to wind up the half open window in the back. The dog, happily panting and oblivious to everything save the mountain scents, lets out a muted yelp as his salivating tongue is wedged into the lip of the window (you have to picture it). Dad flattens the accelerator. Tyres screech, children screech, Cheki dives for cover and the stationwagon disappears in a cloud of smoke.

Frivolity aside, more often than not there is a line of people waiting to have their photographs taken.

Behind the face paint and the bird plumage there is a likeable larrikin, good for a giggle with those who take the time to step out from behind their cameras. Ask Cheki how many people take his photograph a day and he'll tell you straight: "Plenti ol man i stap." Ask him the number and, like many villagers, he'll proudly take you to the limit of his numerical capability – 10, which can mean anything from 10 to 10,000.

After more than a decade on the job, Cheki "savvies" the ways of the white man. He visited Australia once as part of a cultural exchange programme and worked out pretty quickly what it was all about. He tends

Left: Not quite blending in with the scenery, Cheki looks to attract the attention of unsuspecting tourists and charges them two Kina to have their photographs taken next to him. The only thing more colourful than his warlike appearance are the stories tourists tell about him when they get back home with their photographs.

to give as much as he gets, judging accurately the limits of his potential benefactor's ignorance. You laugh a lot and pay him what he deserves and you'll leave with a good photo. Make the mistake of trying to sneak a shot without paying and you'll end up with your head in the spirit house (at least that's what his steely expression would have you believe).

GOROKA SHOW

PREPARATION – CLICKING CAMERAS – A BIT OF HISTORY – TOP TURN OUT – SPECTACULAR FINALE

 As sunlight pierces the early morning mist, the dawn song of the Bird of Paradise echoes the highlands of Papua New Guinea, majestically heralding the start of the 1990 Goroka Show. For the next three days more than a hundred Sing Sing groups from provinces throughout the country will converge at the Eastern Highlands capital for what will be one of the richest and most colourful cultural events in the national calendar.

In the bedrooms and bathrooms of the local hotels, guests who have flown in from all over the world are preparing for the day ahead. Amid the excited chatter, sun blockouts are splashed onto faces, arms and legs. Comfortable walking shoes and a hat are given priority. "You'll be walking around most of the day and don't be fooled by the cool temperature, it's a dangerous sun," warns the guide. Final check: Entry pass, camera, film and some small change for a drink.........better take some more film just in case.

In the restaurant, guests are selecting from an elaborate breakfast buffet of cereals, juices and eggs. "It's going to be a big show because Mt Hagen was cancelled," booms one guest in an American drawl that's echoed the world. "It's coinciding with the country's 15th anniversary celebrations and more than 100,000 people are expected to pass through the gate," adds a German tourist.

Meanwhile, some distance away beside a cluster of smoking thatched huts, another ritual of preparation is nearing completion. Pig grease is being liberally smeared over bodies, and feathers collected and passed down through generations are being meticulously arranged into elaborate headdresses. Huge shell breastplates, as treasured as family jewellery, are secured to torsos; Pandanus leaves are cut and corrugated then inserted to pieces of twine wrapped around the waist. Beneath the colourful bird plumes, brightly coloured paints are applied to faces with painstaking detail – reds and yellows, blues and black. Once created from soils and plant roots, the colourful body paints used today are factory produced in small tins of powder cleverly marketed as "Sing Sing Paint." Handfuls of Taro, Kau Kau (sweet potato) and Banana are eaten to sustain energy throughout the day of dancing.

After final scrutiny of the "Bilas" by family and village elders, the dancers begin singing and pounding their Kundu drums, collecting crowds of spectators as they move forward towards the Goroka Showground.

By 8am the road leading to the cultural arena is a river of bird plumes banked by spectators. Like fireflies at night, hundreds of tiny camera flashes sparkle along its length. At the head of each Sing Sing group a placard is carried to identify the performer's region of origin – Pindiu, Kabwum, Bogia and Sepic. Attracting particular attention are the local Asaro mudmen with their grizzly mud masks of boar teeth, and the Huli Wigmen from the Southern Highland province with their painted yellow faces and hats of human hair. As each group enters the main arena, the line lurches forward and the cacophony of music and singing intensifies. Tourists, oblivious to their waning film, click frantically until the dancers finally spill into the huge arena for the judging.

It was 33 years ago the first Goroka Show was staged. It began primarily as an agricultural exhibition but today it is one of the two biggest cultural

Opposite page: The Goroka Show is a family day for both spectators and performers. At an early age young boys become involved, studying their parents until the day they are able to take their place.

Above: The Huli wigmen capture the attention of the tourists with their bright yellow faces and hats of human hair. In the old days the face paints were made from plant roots and soil. Today, however, performers can buy small cans of cleverly marketed "Sing Sing Paint" from the local store.

Right: The colours used by the performers were often striking, if not by their brightness, then by their design.

events held in the Papua New Guinea highlands (the other being the Mt Hagen Show which was cancelled due to law and order problems.) As well as the Sing Sing competition, the show's three day programme includes drama performances, exhibitions, sporting events and commercial displays. Two recent additions include a display about protecting the environment and the Miss Goroka Show beauty contest.

By 11am the showground oval is transformed into a kaleidoscope of colour teeming with thousands of painted and feathered bodies. From the spectators grandstand the different Sing–Sing groups can be distinguished. There is a cluster of charcoal blackened bodies in hats that are being kept perpetually alight by a man filling them with kerosene. Beside them is a small army of warriors taunting each other in mock battle with bows and arrows. Elephantine women with shell discs threaded through their nose gaze numbly into the audience from brightly painted faces while men in bear–like costumes stagger about on stilts. It's an amazing spectacle, made more fascinating by closer investigation when judging for the day is finished and spectators are allowed to enter the arena and walk among the dancers.

The dancing continues at an exhaustive pace until midday when both

Left & Below: Provinces throughout Papua New Guinea are represented at the show. These women from the Sepik River would be similarly decorated for a ritual in their local village in which their bodies were scarred in homage to the crocodile spirits of the Sepik River.

spectators and performers retreat to the shade to escape the intensity of the sun. Stories are exchanged by tourists eager to prove nothing had been overlooked, and dancers look for assurance that they have won the prizemoney. (A record sum totalling K25,000 (about AUD$35,000) is being offered to the winners in several different categories.)

On the first day the traditional dancing ends early to allow the crowds to visit the stalls and exhibits but the following day it continues well into the afternoon. Towards the end of day three the show is reaching its crescendo. Thousands of dancers are prancing and whirling to individual drumbeats and three metre high headdresses are rolling backwards and forwards in huge waves of colour. As the winning groups are announced, songs and cries of triumph sweep the arena and spectators pour onto the field to join the celebration. Prizes are given in a host of categories to ensure the spirit of the gathering is not lost.

Come dusk the crowds and dancers are making their way back to their villages along the meandering mountain trails as a fine mist envelopes the treetops. Like an empty theatre, the valley again falls still and silent .... but for the closing song of the Bird of Paradise.

Opposite page & Above: The Goroka Showground is transformed into a kaleidoscope of colour teeming with thousands of bodies. The dancing continues at an exhaustive pace during judging, with few in the arena stopping long enough to have their photographs taken.

Above & Left: There was rarely a moment when there was nothing to capture your attention. Whether it was the expressions of delight mixed into the audience that surrounded the judging arena, the huge coloured wings carried on the shoulders of the dancers, or the creativity of the costumes.

Above & Right: Thousands of dancers pranced and whirled to individual drumbeats in stark contrast to the brass band in their midst.

Opposite page & Left: Packed into the arena are hundreds of different bilas. There is a cluster of charcoal blackened bodies with hats that are being kept perpetually alight by a man filling them with kerosene. Dancers from another group are standing on one foot and have moss dangling from their noses. One old woman is wandering through the crowd with an umbrella in her arms, looking as if all the dancing might bring rain.

Above & Left: The performers are good at improvising. Dancers in one group cut bamboo into strips to make talons for their hands. Adding to their grisly appearance, bamboo is also wedged between their nose and their mouth. One highlander demonstrated his political bias by using a political poster in the back of his headdress.

Above & Right: For both the amateur and professional photographer the Goroka Show is unparalleled in its richness of images. It is an exhausting, yet immeasurably rewarding, three day experience in which your biggest single challenge is likely to be not running out of film.

Above: An ignited garbage can was thrown into a car window. Vehicles that lined the streets were extensively damaged by the protesters.

Inset Top: The protesters wreaked havoc as they moved towards Parliament House. Shop windows were smashed, garbage cans were ignited and cars were overturned. Sadly, most of the destruction was caused by a vanguard of youths obviously intent on inciting violence.

Inset Centre: Police managed to repel the 4,000 strong demonstration with few injuries. However, thousands of kina in damage had been caused to shops and vehicles.

Inset Bottom: Contrary to public opinion, not all demonstrations in the national capital end in destruction of property. In a separate demonstration, thousands of students from the University of Papua New Guinea marched on Parliament House protesting about corruption in government. No property was damaged and nobody was injured.

DEMONSTRATION

"PEACE" MARCH – VIOLENT CONFRONTATION – DESERTED MINISTER

There is something unsettling about stepping out of your office and into an oncoming riot of about 3,000 people armed with machetes and iron bars. God knows there are people back home complaining about having to face city crowds.

If I had read the morning paper I would have known about the "peace" march to Parliament House which was to start on a nearby oval. I would have read about the fatal bashing of a young youth leader and the violence Port Moresby residents say is being generated by immigrating Highlanders.

But I didn't and, stepping from my office like it was any other day, I walked straight into 3,000 screaming demonstrators. Something is not quite right I thought as rocks shattered nearby windows and cars were overturned.

From the security of my office (a vantage I returned to with remarkable pace) I watched as the crowd violently spilled through the street. Vehicles were pummelled with clubs, windows were smashed with steel rubbish bins, shops were ransacked and cardboard boxes were set alight and thrown into doorways. Incredibly, there was only a small vanguard causing the destruction but it moved like wildfire, scattering those in front of it and leaving a wake of destruction for the hundreds who followed.

Within an hour the crowd had grown to more than 4,000 and was still moving towards Parliament House. A police force of less than 50 men with tear gas and shotguns had regrouped a short distance ahead and stood in its path. Confrontation was inevitable. As police fired gas canisters into the crowd, pandemonium reigned. One man was killed. It was enough and the demonstrators were suddenly in retreat, taking their frustration out on property as they passed back through the built up area and eventually dispersed.

Despite the obvious concern at the way a public march can turn violent so quickly, I can't help but laugh at Justice Minister Narokobi's involvement as he tried to quell the crowd on several occasions.

Said he when recounting the story: "When I climbed onto the bonnet of the police van to address the crowd the first time, my weight caused the metal to touch the battery terminal. Sparks flew everywhere. I thought the car was going to explode so I dived off and when I got up they were off and running."

The Minister was then shuffled into a police car to head the demonstrators off and alighted shortly after, still shaking from his earlier upset, to attempt another address. Walking towards the then ugly crowd he turned to the two accompanying policemen for moral support.

"They were gone, running in the opposite direction. I could not believe it. So I started running after them. The crowd was right behind me as I tried to get back inside the police vehicle but it kept moving away. I was running alongside the police saying "Stop. I'm the Justice Minister, let me in. But they just kept on driving."

The Minister recounted how he eventually gave up and tried to climb a steel mesh fence to safety.

"It was then I realised I was too heavy to lift my own weight. It was terrifying. Police were firing tear gas into the crowd. It was the first time I have experienced tear gas. I saw a stationary police vehicle and dived into it. What a day!"

SING-SING

HYSTERICAL CROWD – PRIMITIVE BLOOD RITES – SECRET ELIXIR – TRIBAL CONFLICT

It's a spectacular sight – a kaleidoscope of colour and activity as bodies glistening with sweat, leap and prance to an evocative drumbeat, shaking the ground beneath them with the pounding of their feet. The gathering is the culmination of weeks of personal preparation with both men and women undertaking a series of painful bloodletting rites. Men's faces are ceremoniously prepared and marked with razor sharp blades while women splash molten paste on their bodies and, in a primitive and excruciating ritual, tear the hair from their flesh. Once completed, both smear themselves with scented animal oils to make their skins glisten. Customary paints and ornaments are then applied to their bodies with meticulous detail– ochre, browns, blues, blood reds and charcoal black. Heavy ornaments, as well as shells and feathers, are then hung from punctured ear lobes. Animal hides are strapped to their feet and bodies.

Once dressed, they are led to the village meeting house, a sacred place for the initiated where they are scrutinised by the elderly. From the dark, smoke filled corners of the room, clusters of cringing, shadowed figures murmur critically as the brightly coloured newcomers file past in their plumage. It is there those planning to attend the performance undergo their final rite of passage by drinking a secretly concocted elixir of putrid liquid. Those weak and unprepared for the ordeal vomit and fall unconscious to the ground; those who remain standing after several hours depart with the blessing of the community elders.

The actual ceremony can last days and is generally the subject of tremendous organisation. Preparation begins months earlier. Performers have to be secured, food gathered from around the countryside and security arranged.

Sadly, security is a primary concern, with groups from different provinces converging on the one site. Though everyone is checked and disarmed as they enter the grounds, knives and other weapons are smuggled through. Invariably battles start. They are incited by small incidents – an offensive gesture, a dispute apparently settled long ago. But they quickly erupt into large and bloody conflicts in which many are left scarred and maimed.

My television arrived yesterday and as you have probably gathered from the story, I have been watching a rock concert for the past hour. Great reception. Here in Port Moresby we receive two direct channel broadcasts from Australia – Queensland Television (Channel 9) and the ABC. And if you're living in the right suburb you can also be hooked up to cable television which gives you two video channels as well as American, Tahitian or Malayan television. Cost: about K30 a month.

But it's funny. I'd almost forgotten what an open air concert back home was like – the preparation, the crowded venues, the clothing, stopping off at the pub on the way and the gang fights that often brought them to a close.

They reckon it's fairly primitive up here........but I guess that really depends on how you look at it.

Opposite Page: It's a kaleidoscope of colour and activity as bodies glistening with sweat leap and prance to an evocative drumbeat.

SILLY SIREN

TOP POSITION – OUT TO LUNCH –
FOLLOWED HOME – OPINION

I met an expatriate woman today who is likely to be sacked and deported or worse still, beaten and raped. Slim and attractive with long blond hair, she's about 24 years old and wears her years with brash confidence. A university degree coupled with an uncommon assertiveness for a woman in a developing country has seen her well placed in government hierarchy and her status has obviously allowed her a voice in the senior decision making process. In a western nation, however, her comments would be drowned out in a murmur of mediocrity.

It is her first time out of England and she is serving a two year contract as an advisor to a national ministry. After only four months in PNG, the fascination her seniors hold for her carefree attitude has found her a popular addition to the office – although that is currently in doubt.

"I had a senior government secretary take me out to lunch the other day and he "laid it on me", she said "I just laughed and told him to forget it. I told a few friends back at the office what happened and now every man and his dog knows. He's lost a lot of face and I've gained it so he's making life a bit difficult at the moment."

In a culture where traditionally women have virtually no say or status, it is incomprehensible to a Melanesian man - certainly a senior bureaucrat - that a woman could cause such embarrassment. He, she says, tried to get her transferred to another office but she refused, no doubt challenging him publicly in the process.

It was a weekend when we met and she was undecided about what to do that Saturday night. "There are a couple of parties on but I'm still recovering from the one last night, and I'm off to the Yacht Club for the Commodore's sail past tomorrow. Thing's are pretty hectic. It's great. No, I don't believe it (PNG) is anywhere near as dangerous as people make out. I'm not scared to walk around at night. I was at a party recently and an expatriate offered to follow me home for safety. I told him not to bother but he insisted. While we were on our way I thought I'd freak him out and pulled into one of the Tucker Boxes (roadside shops) to buy some cigarettes and talk with the men. It's all part of mixing with the culture. I reckon it's the element of surprise that makes it safe. I was in bare feet and a normal dress. It really blew them out. The guy following me grabbed me by the arm and blasted the daylights out of me. It was unbelievable how much he was over-reacting."

It's a sad truth that this woman's greatest crime is her naivety. To some degree it's understandable given the time she has been here, her age and her background. In England her attitude is probably typical of many 24 year old women. But in PNG it is dangerous.

Personally, I am not anywhere near as critical of her as I am of the idiots who sent her here. It has taken one conversation to assess she is a danger to herself as well as her position, and that she shouldn't be in Papua New Guinea with such an attitude.

Who is responsible for recruiting foreign staff to PNG? Who will be answerable if - and let's hope it doesn't happen - she becomes one of the victims we read about in the papers?

No doubt if it does happen, Papua New Guinea's lawlessness will be held to blame........instead of the fools who chose her to come here.

Right & Opposite page: Under the big top of Parliament House, the process of government grinds to a standstill as the country awaits the outcome of another vote of no confidence.

NO CONFIDENCE

MELBOURNE CUP – LOBBYING BEGINS – ABDUCTED POLITICIANS – THE BIG RACE THAT NEVER WAS

Political pundits say they would have a better chance of picking the winner of today's Melbourne Cup than gambling on the outcome of tomorrow's vote of no confidence.

A week ago the Opposition party, led by ousted Prime Minister Pious Wingti, tabled its intentions to replace the 17 month old Namaliu Government. Though the vote of no confidence made the front pages of local newspapers, the details were hardly new. "Wingti has the numbers" roared the headlines. "Namaliu confident" countered the response.

The tabling of the vote of no–confidence signals the beginning of an unusual and entertaining seven day lobbying process to secure the majority of 109 members of Parliament. It's not your western style campaign with politicians moving among the masses, plucking babies from the crowds and assuring little old ladies their pensions are safe. It's the MP's – as representatives of the people – who are wooed and it's not babies they're looking to have kissed. Follow the papers and you will see the transparent efforts of a host of political opportunists swearing their allegiance to one party or another. It's an all in, no holds barred war of words involving MPs, businessmen, would–be politicians, environmentalists, community leaders – you name it. Even the Church has a say, extolling one party's greater

Christian virtues until the media, buckling under a plethora of pontificating press releases, appeal to MP's to cease or improve the standard of their material as most of it is ending up in the bin.

Mingle at the expatriate bars after work and study the one–up–manship of those claiming inside information or direct links with senior ministers. They whisper just loud enough to be heard, gesture just enough to attract attention and allude to knowledge almost enough to warrant credibility. At the hob–nob restaurants while most outside politics have their heads down eating, there are those with their heads up either looking to be seen or to see who is eating with whom. If knowledge is power, gossip is gold.

In an effort to be impartial, the media devote equal and considerable space and air time to both sides of politics. What the media won't use is generally the subject of costly full page advertisements in the newspapers. In the lead up to this vote of no confidence, Wingti led with an eye–catching photograph of several shops destroyed in a recent riot and accused the Government of being unwilling to take responsibility for this country's law and order problems. The next day Namaliu responded with: "My government has never seen the value of such advertisements but we feel this response to the opposition's attack of yesterday is justified."....and also went on to cover a full page.

As the day of the vote nears, lobbying and hearsay intensifies with everyone claiming they can accurately gauge the numbers. The front page of one of the papers has a daily tally by "sources on the inside."

In the corridors of Parliament there is an air of self-importance. MP's from around the country are being wooed by both sides of politics. There are chauffeured cars to meet them as they arrive at the airport, whisking them away to clandestine locations to swear their oaths of allegiance.

Of course around vote of no confidence time Parliament echoes with stories of corruption and intrigue–briberies paid and ministerial portfolios pledged. It is the artful party leader that offers gain by implication, as if it was promised. Two days before the vote, the Namaliu government brought down its second budget and with it considerable controversy outside the House as each of the 109 members of Parliament had their "slush funds" (what the government calls the money needed by MP's to fulfil their electoral responsibilities) increased from K50,000 a year to K100,000.) "This government is not buying votes," expounded Namaliu to an unprecedented silence on the floor of Parliament.

By the time Parliament met to consider the vote it was all back on as MP's took their positions at the barricades, ready for the big race. Namaliu – the favourite– was odds on at 54 to 52 (There were three vacancies) but, as even the most seasoned punters conceded, there was no telling who would win until it was all over. In the members gallery the Whose Who of PNG politics scrutinised the contenders from their privileged positions. (Each MP was only allowed three guests). Amid the excitement and tension, the Speaker called together the field. Throughout the country thousands anxiously tuned into their radios awaiting the outcome. Television cameras were poised ready to transmit the news around the world. Hundreds clamoured at the gates of Parliament.

Then, in the land of the unexpected, the unexpected: Wingti was scratched from the race when his party realised it couldn't muster the numbers and withdrew its vote. Bravado swept the chamber. Insults and challenges were exchanged by contenders on both sides of the floor but regardless, the race was never run and despite extended rumblings to the contrary, life continues much the same as it did before.

I should have paid more attention to the experienced punters who suggested the only way to win is to place a bet each way and save my real gambling for the horses.

INVISIBILITY

BAD LUCK FOR BLACK CATS – MORE SORCERER'S SECRETS – BELIEVE IT OR NOT

So you want to become invisible huh?

Well, according to the sorcerers of the Wampur tribe in the Morobe Province where the ritual of invisibility is still practised, it's easy. Just take one black cat – jet black without any discolouration to the fur – and cut its throat. Be careful that it is unaware of your intention. If it resists the ritual will be unsuccessful. Then cut its paws, wrap the body in a clean cloth and bury it.

There are incantations to be repeated (you didn't expect it all to be revealed by an expatriate pen did you?) and then leave it. Time: years, or at least as long as it takes for the flesh to rot leaving only the bones.

With the lengthy preparation out of the way, exhume the bones and sort them into small piles, hover over a flat body of water so you can see your reflection (nowadays a mirror is easier) and one by one hold the cat's bones between your teeth. Somewhere in that tiny pile that was your furry feline lies the secret to invisibility – a single bone that will make you disappear right in front of your reflection. The sorcerers swear by it.

If you have trouble with the idea of hacking up your black cat, all is not lost as there is an alternative. In Papua New Guinea there is a rare bird that nests on the beaches (the name, like the incantation, was not imparted). Once you have located its nest, take the egg and, as with the bone of the black cat, place it delicately between your teeth. The moment it is secured, poof, you're invisible. It's as easy as that.

However, like all great secrets, bird egg invisibility comes with a catch. If the egg breaks while it is in your mouth, you're invisible for life!

Believe it or not.

SPAK BRUS

DRUGS: GOOD IDEA – COFFEE – THE THREAT

It was about five years ago foreign advisers wandered into the highlands of Papua New Guinea recommending landowners form co-operatives and begin planting coffee. The theory: several landowners get together and raise a sizeable deposit for a bank loan. They work the land and three years later the profits begin to percolate.

At the time it seemed like a good idea. Coffee prices were high in line with world demand and there was ample land to farm. Landowners were motivated as they could see coffee dynasties popping up everywhere and, after all, these educated white men obviously knew what they were talking about.

It would be three years until the first harvest they said. No repayments were required by the banks until then, by which time the landowners would have more than enough money to start paying back the loan...........at least that was the theory.

Three years later, however, there was a slump in coffee prices and despite a bountiful harvest founded on hard work and expectation, the landowners barely saw a return. Three years for what they asked? Instead of growing taro which they could eat and trade, they had grown coffee which was of virtually no worth to them.

It all seemed grossly unfair. Of course there were students, politicians and businessmen who understood world commodities but they were not the ones that had been promised more money to buy pigs and sugar. To add to the dilemma, three years were up and the landowners had to start repaying their loans – either that or lose their land.

Understandably they were a touch perturbed.

In response the banks provided bridging finance for two years (It was certainly a low-risk option compared to trying to claim the land from the traditional landowners.) and the landowners, with little choice, returned to the land to grow coffee.

Today marks the passing of the fifth year since the landowners began growing coffee. Prices are still rockbottom and the banks are again threatening to foreclose. In a desperate bid to prop up the ailing coffee industry, the government has injected millions of kina into it hoping world prices will eventually improve. It has become a waiting game in which – after five years – few have any alternative but to play along.

But this story is not about Coffee, it's about Marijuana and a situation which is contributing to Papua New Guinea's escalating law and order problem – particularly in the highlands where you pay less for a "joint" than you do for a cigarette.

Put yourself in the position of one of those landowners when someone comes along and suggests you can re-plant a fraction of your land with Spak Brus (marijuana) and make five or 10 times the amount of money you were promised from the coffee in just six months. With the money you make, you can pay back the bank, keep your land and still grow your coffee if you want to. Sure it's illegal but what choice have you got? And anyway, who is going to know? The police aren't organised enough to find it and your wantoks aren't going to tell. The alternative is to lose your land and where will that leave you? Here's K500 downpayment.

It is so frighteningly simple and it's happening.

But then, what would you do if you were in the landowner's position?

COMIC COUP

SACKED COMMISSIONER – HUMAN TRAGEDY
THE BOUGAINVILLE FACTOR

There was a coup attempt in Port Moresby last night.

Police Commissioner Paul Tohian incited the assembly of the capital's police and defence force to march on Parliament House and overthrow the government. Drunk on a combination of alcohol and stories of Fiji's General Rambuka, the Commissioner intended to place the Prime Minister and members of the cabinet under house arrest but despite the call to arms of police and defence forces he was the only one who turned up for the show.

He was sacked the next day.

It was an undignified conclusion to the 20 year career of one of the country's most distinguished policemen – recipient of the Queen's Police Medal, Controller of the Bougainville State of Emergency and commander of numerous police special operations for which he received the highest of commendations.

The media today gave details of the Commissioner's demise. The attempted coup started early yesterday afternoon with a series of celebrations for servicemen returning from Bougainville – first at Murray Barracks then at Taurama Barracks. According to the Prime Minister's later statement, it was during these two functions the Commissioner – while heavily under the influence of liquor – attempted to incite Defence Force personnel. The reports went on to say the Commissioner left the function and used his police car radio to order policemen onto standby ready to overthrow the government. In a call to arms, Tohian said he was moving on Parliament House but arrived to find the area deserted. Desperate, he raced to McGregor and then Gordon Barracks where he ordered policemen into combat gear.

Meanwhile, at Boroko Police Station, three senior officers had managed to convince a large body of police and defence personnel not to have anything to do with the coup. When the Commissioner arrived at the Boroko station he was unable to win the confidence of the crowd. He was drunk; there was uncertainty and confusion in the ranks. According to the reports, he was then "calmed down and driven home."

Behind the obvious error of judgement lies a story of considerable human tragedy.

Prior to his involvement in Bougainville, Paul Tohian was known as a first rate policeman able to handle the toughest of situations. He was the man that could be trusted to do the job when nothing else worked – the Papua New Guinea version of John Wayne who went into the toughest situations with guns blazing and brought everything under control. But it is important to remember his talents were always that of a sergeant – not a general; his job was to win the battle, not the war.

Tohian specialised in public order upheavals – tribal fighting in the highlands, student protests at the national university, prison riots at Bomana and the state of emergency in the National Capital District. He was well respected by the men under his command.

As controller of the State of Emergency on Bougainville, Tohian found himself and his actions the subject of both public and international scrutiny. In the past he struck fast and hard, bringing the situation rapidly to an end before questions needed to be answered. But Bougainville was different – it was political. Tohian's objective was to crush the militant uprising but every time he got close, his political masters intervened, seeking compromise with the militants instead of capitulation. The situation under his control dragged on for more than eight months. Public pressure for a solution increased as the numbers of dead rose. While politicians debated the pros and cons of their decisions, Tohian remained the man in the public spotlight. Church groups and the media began to criticise police and defence forces on Bougainville for their brutality. Human rights became the issue as frustrated servicemen lashed out at a situation for which they were not trained or able to change. The militants were getting the upper hand simply because they continued to exist and there was nothing Tohian and his men could do about it.

Commuting between Bougainville and Port Moresby to report to the National Executive Council, Tohian started to publicly vent his frustration under the pressure of a questioning and demanding public who knew him as a man of action. At a local watering hole he was reportedly seen drunk, wielding a firearm, and threatening to put a bullet through the militant leader's head. Shortly after the coup attempt, hearsay said Tohian had been planning for three weeks to take over the government to allow him to deal with the Bougainville situation unhampered by the politicians.

It was three weeks before the attempted coup that Namaliu ordered the armed forces out of Bougainville so the government could again negotiate with the militants. Tohian argued that police and defence forces shouldn't be pulled out and that if they were, it was dangerous to leave a small police force which was unable to defend itself against the militants, should negotiations break down. The government ignored him and he ignored the government, pulling all police out of Bougainville regardless.

Right: A mock battle was staged to relieve the tension as people from the lower Kagul Valley waited to see if the tribes they had fought for more than six months would attend the peace ceremony. Warriors divided into two opposing groups and fired arrows and bullets over each other's heads.

PEACE CEREMONY

TRIBAL FIGHT – MOCK BATTLE – DEVASTATION – EPILOGUE OR PRELUDE

NAME: Lo Nepawa
AGE: About 45
CLAN: Tendepo
DISTRICT: Tambul
MARITAL STATUS: Married with one wife and seven children
CAUSE OF DEATH: Died instantly when shotgun pellets entered forehead and came out the back of the head, damaging his brain.

NAME: Kundi Kama
AGE: 49
CLAN: Kepaka
DISTRICT: Tambul
MARITAL STATUS: Married with two children
CAUSE OF DEATH: Gun shot and axe wounds

And so began the official report by the Western Highlands Provincial Government that ended a six month tribal fight in which 28 men were killed, hundreds injured and thousands of kina in damage was caused to property and business throughout the Kagul valley.

The conflict started with a drunken fight and a murder. Six months later, after an alleged payback killing, it had escalated into a pitched battle that divided the Kagul valley and involved more than 4,000 warriors of the Kavaga, Sipakau, Yano and Yapkulumind clans. In the middle of the valley a one kilometre stretch of land became a permanent battlefield, bordered at both sides by huge barricades and ditches that blockaded the only supply road. Warriors manned the barriers day and night, at times breaching the enemy frontier to raid nearby villages.

But now the hill on which the battles had been fought was the site for the peace ceremony. A makeshift platform had been erected from which clan leaders and dignitaries would make their speeches. Thousands of people from throughout the valley were expected to attend.

Preparation for the ceremony began early in the morning as warriors in traditional bilas came together and began the several kilometre march to the site. In the lower Kagul, hundreds of men, women and children joined the procession, eventually arriving at the base of the hill where they waited to be led forward by the mediators. As they waited, however, the tension mounted. Six weeks had been spent negotiating peace with leaders from both sides of the valley but the clans from the upper Kagul had lost 15 men to the lower Kagul's 13 and had not fully embraced the peace plan. Many people from the lower Kagul were hopeful for an end to the fighting, but few were confident. To relieve the tension, the main body of warriors divided into two groups and faced each other in mock battle, firing arrows overhead and shooting bullets into the air. With each shot, several men dropped as if struck, and performed a dramatic – though lingering – death while the onlookers roared their delight.

According to Father Joseph Bisson of the Kiripia Catholic Mission, the conflict had been particularly bloody and most people in the valley were anxious to see it ended. Firearms – high powered rifles and home made shotguns – had quickly replaced traditional weapons such as axes, spears

Above: Warriors from the lower Kagul Valley marched several kilometres, growing in numbers as they neared the battlefield on which 13 of their men had been killed.

Right: A young man sits in the charred remains of his home near the barricade which divided the Kagul Valley. He watched as his father was hacked to death by members of a raiding party.

Far Right: Barricades were erected around villages to protect their people from the raiding parties. Ditches were dug, corrugated iron was propped up by boulders and young men (pictured) stood on standby, ready to repel the invaders.

Below: Farmers left their families to man the barricades and defend their land. For weeks on end they lived in small humpies such as this awaiting the onslaught of the opposition.

Far Left: Anna Dopo tends her husband's grave. Gerard Dopo was the first victim in the tribal fight that divided the Kagul Valley.

Left & Below: Caught in the middle. Having lost her son in the fighting, this old woman tends his grave while the fighting continued around her.

STATUTORY DECLARATION

PAPUA NEW GUINEA

I, (a) _____, Councillor and Village Leader of _____

clan of _____ tribe, Lower/Kagul.

do solemnly and sincerely declare that (b)

1/ Will not incite any more tribal fighting involving my clan/tribe.

2/ Will not allow my clansmen to murder anyone from Lower/Upper Kagul.

3/ Will do everything possible to normalise our relationship with people from Lower/Upper Kagul.

4/ This current tribal fight resulting 28 deaths is now ended today Thursday 15 March 1990

5/ In breach of this agreement Police must move in and raid my village and arrest me.

And I make this solemn declaration by virtue of the *Oaths, Affirmations and Statutory Declarations Ordinance 1962* conscientiously believing the statements contained therein to be true in every particular.

Declared at .... (c) ....
Before me—
the ....day of (d) ....
..........................19..... (c) ....

(a) Here insert name, address and occupation of person making the declaration.
(b) Here insert the matter declared to. Where the matter is long, it should be set out in numbered paragraphs.
(c) Signature of person making the declaration.
(d) Signature of person before whom the declaration is made.
(e) Here insert title of person before whom the declaration is made.

NOTE:— Any person who wilfully makes a false statement in a Statutory Declaration is guilty of an indictable offence, and is liable to imprisonment, with or without hard labour, for four years.

Above: A standard government form was used to signify the end of the tribal battle...." In breach of this agreement police must move in and raid my village and arrest me."

and bows and arrows. The Mission has an aid centre which, in father Joseph's words, "was turned into a virtual M.A.S.H unit as the injured and dead were brought in". With the road to Mt Hagen blockaded, the mission provided the only medical service to the hundreds of injured on the lower Kagul side of the valley.

"The sisters were working around the clock over Christmas. We had men and boys as young as 14 years old, being brought in with shocking injuries – arrow, spear and shotgun wounds. There was one man who had been shot five times and had half his head blown away. Another I could have fitted my fist into the hole in his chest."

Father Bisson, who has been in the area 26 years and whose mission lies in the lower Kagul Valley, holds the clan leaders of the upper Kagul and police primarily responsible for the extent of the damage.

"The clan leaders from the upper Kagul asked for 10,000 kina and 1,000 pigs in compensation for the first death of the fight. It was an unrealistic demand but still the people of the lower Kagul were seeking to meet it because they didn't want a war. But before they had a chance to raise the compensation, raiding parties of the opposing clan struck."

According to Father Bisson, the fight plunged the entire region into chaos as food and supplies dwindled. "Schools were closed down and crops were forgotten as subsistence farmers took up arms to fight. Trade stores and houses were burnt to the ground. With no supplies coming into the area, people were starving. We had children coming to the mission who could barely walk," he said.

Father Bisson says he and his mission were threatened by people of the upper Kagul who resented the service they were providing the injured warriors. "We didn't get involved in the fight at all but to help the injured, yet messages came back to me saying that if it continued I would have been killed. I never went anywhere near the battle zone and since the fight started, I haven't been into the upper Kagul area although that's part of my parish. The police also exacerbated the situation and should be made accountable for the widespread destruction they caused in what they claimed was an effort to stop the tribal fighting," he said.

By noon, more than 2,000 people of the lower Kagul waited at the top of the hill. Dignitaries were seated – the Premier, several MP's and church leaders – but the clans from the upper Kagul had still not arrived. The wait continued, an hour passed.

Then they appeared. Hundreds of men ran onto the hill from the opposite side, singing and yelling with weapons still in hand. The clansmen from the lower Kagul jumped to their feet and also began yelling while government mediators frantically ran from one group to the other to settle the crowd. Eventually the leaders from both sides came forward and sat on the ground. Those behind them did likewise until silence ensued.

About a thousand warriors from both the lower and upper Kagul sat facing each other while the leaders talked about their losses and swore an end to the conflict. But there was still an air of tension. Peace ceremonies are well known for ending in violence over an apparently minor gesture or a misconstrued parable. There was one particularly anxious moment. It occurred when one chief was interrupted by another and confusion was apparent over who should speak next. Clan members of both sides rose to their feet and gestured their disapproval as both leaders sought to speak above the other, but mediators managed to contain the situation. Two large pigs and a mountain of rice were given by Provincial government representatives to the paramount chiefs to seal the agreement.

Finally statutory declarations were signed and hands were shaken, formally – though far from certainly – ending the conflict.

Left: The opposing clans, now seated on the ground , faced one another while their leaders talked about the loss and suffering that had resulted from the battle. The people of the Upper Kagul valley demonstrated their anger at police with placards accusing them of being responsible for most of the destruction throughout the valley.

Left: After addressing the crowd for several hours, paramount chiefs and provincial dignitaries signed and witnessed a statutory declaration agreeing that the fighting was over.

TRIBAL FIGHTING

BACKGROUND – WHY FIGHT – THE WEAPONS – FIGHTING TECHNIQUES – THEN AND NOW – A HIGHLANDER'S VIEW – THE ALTERNATIVES

 Tribal fighting has long been a means for solving clan disputes in Papua New Guinea.

Historically, tribal warfare was practised throughout the country well before white settlement in the early 19th century but colonial administration saw it harshly suppressed – particularly in the coastal and island regions which were easily accessible by water. It wasn't until the 1930's that colonial authority penetrated the highlands and outlawed tribal fighting in the region. For 20 years Kiaps (patrol officers) successfully policed the area using firearms to keep fighting to a minimum.

However, the advent of a more liberal and democratic legal system in the 1960's and the country's independence in the 1970's led to the deterioration of state mechanisms for resolving inter–tribal disputes. Unlike the people of the coastal regions, highlanders had only a few decades without tribal fighting and those who had fought previously still remembered it as an appropriate means for solving dispute. Consequently, there was a resurgence of tribal warfare in the highlands, which is apparent today.

There are three main types of tribal fights – the large full–scale battles where as many as 8,000 armed warriors from two major clans meet at a designated area and fight for months on end; the inter–clan battles, where smaller clans fight to expand their territory or dominate one another; and the small–scale payback clan battles which tend to be characterised by raiding party skirmishes involving up to 20 men.

REASONS

What actually starts a tribal fight is often hard to determine, though conflicts primarily stem from disputes between clans over land, payback killings, women, pigs and sorcery. Often the real reason for fighting is hidden and disputes which were resolved more than a decade passed, can be re–ignited by a seemingly innocent comment or insignificant gesture.

Clan alliance in the highlands is incredibly complex, and the bond between one clan and another can span generations. From the days when small villages joined to protect one another against their enemies, clan loyalty has been paramount in communal Melanesian society. A fight between two small sub–clans can quickly escalate to involve several major clans on both sides, each considering it their duty to participate. From such commitments, obligations are met and new ones forged, sometimes involving thousands of people.

Because of the linguistic diversity of the highland people and the fact they often speak in parables, it is difficult to interpret the subtleties of the communication between groups and the traditional significance of what is being said. A comment considered a joke by one group, for example, can be perceived as an insult by another and reflect on an entire clan, particularly if the individuals involved are from clans that are traditional enemies. It is likely, however, that the insult is just an excuse to re–start a conflict in which one side was dissatisfied with the outcome of a previous settlement.

Opposite page: For many of the young boys in the village, tribal fighting was a big adventure, but they learnt quickly that it was not a game. Regardless of their age - many barely teenagers - once they were on the battlefield they became the enemy and were allowed no quarter.

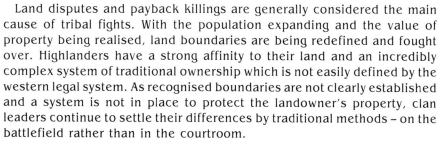

Land disputes and payback killings are generally considered the main cause of tribal fights. With the population expanding and the value of property being realised, land boundaries are being redefined and fought over. Highlanders have a strong affinity to their land and an incredibly complex system of traditional ownership which is not easily defined by the western legal system. As recognised boundaries are not clearly established and a system is not in place to protect the landowner's property, clan leaders continue to settle their differences by traditional methods – on the battlefield rather than in the courtroom.

The attitude "An eye for an eye" has always rated highly in the minds of highlanders and traditionally, clan members are obliged – not to the dead but to the living – to avenge the death or honour of one of their brothers in arms. As a result, payback killings often occur immediately, or many years later, even down through the generations. Each death – whether directly or indirectly associated with an opposing clan – can result in renewed tribal conflict.

Women are often the centre of tribal fight disputes – bride price settlements, jealously and marriage disagreements being the main causes. Sorcery too is blamed. A man's death or injury, poor crops or any major misfortune can all be interpreted as signs of an enemy sorcerer's magic. As pigs are the paramount sign of wealth in the highlands, the death or theft of a pig is also reason enough to start a battle.

Offering some insight into the reasons given for starting a tribal fight is the following extract of a report compiled by the Enga Provincial Government from 1976 to 1982.

Immediate Cause of Fight	Number of fights	Deaths Reported
Marriage Problems	9	2
Land and Garden Ownership	22	14
Theft or Dispute over pigs	16	2
Compensation Payments	5	0
Insults	2	0
Thefts (other than pigs)	2	6
Deaths	24	19
Election/Political Meeting	3	0
Wilful Damage	5	0
Public Building Damage	2	0
Moka/Debt arrangements	2	0
Court Decision	2	0
Other	6	0
Not known	22	14
TOTAL	124	57

Left: Police armouries are packed with weapons confiscated from tribal fights. As the armouries are filled, the weapons are taken out and burnt. There have been incidents where police arsenals have been broken into and rifles stolen.

WEAPONS

Today, weapons used in tribal fighting include the bow and arrow, the spear and shield, the axe or machete and – more recently – wartime firearms and home made shotguns.

The bow is about a metre and a half in length and is made of Black Palm, a naturally laminated wood that's particularly strong and flexible. A flat bamboo strip or length of rattan acts as the bow–string and is capable of propelling the arrow up to 60 metres. The arrows are thin strips of sharpened cane grass, hardened by fire. Some can be more elaborate, barbed and grooved to snap on impact or weighted with hollowed human bones filled with poisons. Sometimes the head of the arrow is sheathed in the claw of a Cassowary which on impact remains in the wound to fester, causing the victim to suffer a lingering and painful death.

Like the bows, the spears are made of Black Palm and are about three and a half metres in length. They are borne by warriors carrying body length shields and are used more as a stabbing instrument than a projectile. Forming a defensive front line, several shield bearers move forward for close contact battle, dodging and darting from their opponent's lunge.

The axe or machete is a common fighting tool. Rarely will you see a warrior in battle without one dangling from his side. Though previously made from obsidian and wood, the axe is now more likely to be metal and readily purchased from a trade store. It is used in close contact combat, mostly in raiding party skirmishes. In some parts of the highlands, warriors also use a light fighting pick – similar to an axe but with a Cassowary claw instead of a blade – which they wield in flight.

The highland's wartime history saw thousands of firearms scattered throughout the region and today, many of them, particularly Point 303 and Point 22 rifles, are still used in tribal conflict with devastating effect – both on the enemy and the users as many have proved defective in actual use. Modern firearms are also stolen from police armouries. Ammunition – if not re–cycled from spent cartridges – is being smuggled into the region and includes "dum dum" shells that explode on impact (cost: up to K30 a bullet). Home made firearms are now commonplace on the highland battlefield. Styles vary, though typical are shotguns fashioned from wood, water pipe, cord and a primitive firing mechanism such as a small door latch drawn by heavy duty rubber.

FIGHTING TECHNIQUES

Staying alive at the front line of traditional tribal conflicts is not easy. Following are fighting techniques passed on to me by fight leaders and gleaned from the works of studying academics:

- Don't waste arrows aiming for the head; always aim at the body.
- Pick out a single opponent.
- Note how many arrows your opponent has left and be ready to leap in with axe or spear when his supply is exhausted.
- Don't ever turn your back on the enemy.
- Never fire all your arrows. Always keep one to draw as you drop back.
- Do not start to dodge until your enemy draws his bow to the point of release. Then he will have difficulty in aiming again.
- An archer normally holds the bow in the left hand and pulls the arrow with the right, therefore the shot has a tendency to swing to the left.
- If you can see the shaft of your enemy's arrow in flight, remain still and that arrow will miss you. If you cannot see the shaft duck or dodge.
- If an arrow hits you keep your eyes on the enemy as you drop back to safety. Do not distract the man beside you by asking him for help.
- Listen for the signals of the older men and the fight leaders and go at once as they direct you.
- Bend low but keep your ass behind the shield or you'll get it shot off.

THEN AND NOW

Tribal fighting in the highlands today has changed dramatically from what it was in the early 1900's. The "Lapuns" (old men) say there is no honour any more. In the old days, tribal fights were well organised and controlled by community leaders with traditional sanctions agreed upon by the opposing clans. When tribal fights were declared, women and children were not harmed. Today young children are killed and women are brutally raped to show a man's contempt for his enemy. In the old days when bows and arrows were used, injuries and deaths were few in relation to the numbers of people involved in the fighting. Today, however, modern weapons are resulting in many more deaths and far more serious injuries. With modern communication and transportation, the clan alliance system has expanded. Greater numbers are taking part in the fighting and challenges are more frequent.

New reasons for starting a tribal fight have also developed as one culture begins to merge with another exerting new social and economic pressures on the community. Education is challenging traditional values that once controlled warfare, and alcohol is fuelling aggression in a people well known for their fiery temperament. Today one of the greatest single contributors to starting tribal fights is road accident deaths.

In the 1990's raiding party style conflict is more common. In the past, a site for the battle was agreed upon by both parties and ample notice was given to prepare. A large traditional tribal fight used to have all the makings of a grand final football match. Spectators from both clans would sit on ridges overlooking the battle and cheer their clansmen in safety. Now, again with the advent of high-powered rifles, anyone seen in the vicinity of the opposition is easy prey to the marksmen. No longer does one warrior meet another in the field of combat, satisfied just to end a fight with honour. Today warriors move in groups, depending more on surprise than skill, to inflict maximum damage to both life and property. In past battles, when a man was injured, his enemies would allow his fellow clansmen to move him to safety. Now they stampede their opponents and mutilate the victim's body. No longer is the advice of clan leaders listened to by the young men who have found different ways to win their battles.

Left: Spears and shields are used in the front line of the battle. Opponents will come within striking distance of each other and weave then thrust until one of the spears finds its mark.

Below: The trade store axe or machete and the home made shotgun are becoming increasingly prevalent in tribal warfare. Home made shotguns are constructed from pieces of water pipe and wood.
The firing mechanisms are made from door latches, bits of umbrella and lengths of tyre rubber.

Left: Despite police efforts, tribal fighting continues in the highlands, causing widespread damage to property, loss of life and injury. Bows and arrows and axes are still widely used in tribal warfare, though the advent of modern firearms World War Two rifles and home-made shot guns - has led to an alarming increase in the number of deaths and injuries.

Above: Young boys - barely able to pull a bow - are often involved in the tribal fighting. They carry pieces of corrugated tin to protect their bodies. For many of the boys it is all a game, an opportunity to demonstrate their manhood.

Opposite page: The bow and arrow is still the most common weapon in tribal fighting as it is easily produced. A variety of arrows are used, most honed from sharpened cane grass. Some arrows are made from the bone of a human forearm and are guided by sorcery to ensure they hit their mark. Others are tipped with the claw of a Cassowary, causing the victim to suffer a lingering and painful death.

HIGHLANDER'S VIEW

Contrary to western perception that tribal fighting is a law and order problem, highlanders involved in the fighting see it as a means to instil law and order in their community. Says the 1984 Clifford Report on law and order: "In some circumstances, highlanders turn to tribal fighting not to create disorder but to make their relationships with others more satisfactory or more orderly. Tribal fighting is a response to disorder. For participants, the law and order problem is the offence or the dispute, not the fighting."

To many highlanders, clan warfare is not only a means of solving dispute but a way to bond communities together, strengthen individual relationships and create alliances with other clans. As communities come together against a common enemy, new ties are forged. They become reliant on one another, well beyond the period of conflict.

On an individual level, a fight is a warrior's opportunity to demonstrate his strength and bring honour to his family and clan. Says Kama Kerpi, a highlander whose university field study was on clan wars in the Chimbu Province between 1974–75: "To stand for the clan at times of grave peril was regarded as the highest duty of every clansman. There was dignity in their actions and since these were done to secure their women, their children and their land, warfare was justified. A man was very seriously committed to his action which was something positive and dynamic, leaving virtually no room for forces like boredom, laziness, apathy and psychological strain to destroy one's dignity."

ALTERNATIVES

Papua New Guinea has produced numerous publications on how to end tribal fighting disputes, the Paney Report of 1973 being one of the most comprehensive.

The report set the scene for 1973 "While the actual number of reported fights may not have increased greatly, the number of people involved in those fights, the number of people killed and wounded, the amount of damage done to property and the ferocity with which the fights were pursued, have all increased markedly."

As a solution, Paney advocated traditional methods for solving disputes be incorporated into Papua New Guinea's justice system. He recommended traditional mediators become involved in solving disputes, that ties be strengthened between the police and the community, and that greater emphasis be placed on improved education and business opportunities throughout the community. Sorcery, he says, should be treated seriously, compensation claims paid immediately – possibly through a government insurance fund that prevents dangerous delays in payments –, "core" clans should be held liable for starting a fight, and onus should be placed on individuals of clans to prove they were not involved in the dispute, or be deemed guilty.

Paney's punishment for being found guilty of taking part in a tribal fight: Hard labour imprisonment, parole work in effected area, group pig fines and compensation.

Now, some 15 years after the Paney Report was published, it's interesting to observe what is happening in the Eastern, Western and Southern Highland Provinces, Enga and Chimbu.

Possibly the greatest deterrent to tribal fighting today is the police force which deals with it "The highland way". If a fight erupts, police go in and tell everyone to stop or they will return, burn all their houses down, uproot their crops and kill their pigs. As one senior officer said: "We burn down their houses to keep them busy. They haven't got time to fight if they are re-building their houses and planting new crops." Invariably the warning goes unheeded but it doesn't take long for the community to get the hint. In the short-term, the Police Department's objective is realised – the fighting stops. In the longer term, however, the method is a major concern, not only in relation to human rights which are being abused, but because it is ostracizing the police force from the community. Bear in mind too, that this only applies to communities that are accessible by road. The rest of the highlands are still left to sort the problem out for themselves.

The Justice Department has moved to strengthen the relationship between the community and the village court system as a way of solving the dispute before it reaches tribal fight proportions. To some degree, it is successful. Mediators now move to liaise with clan leaders to negotiate settlement, and highland provincial governments are supporting the initiative. However, there is little real rapport between the police, justice and correctional service systems which, to a large degree, are pulling against one another. Police are focusing on enforcement of western law while the court system is seeking to promote traditional methods of settlement and encourage community based policing.

In the long-term, education and economic development appear to be the most realistic solutions to the problem. With improvement of the legal system and increased community confidence in its ability to solve disputes, clans may look to the legal system as an alternative to fighting. Improvement of education standards and communication will also have an impact as communities become increasingly aware of the futility and destruction caused by tribal fighting.

Left & Below: "The highland way" Chimbu police said people in the community were harbouring stolen firearms, so they moved in, tearing up crops and razing village huts.

Above: Boys are taught to sharpen their reflexes for the day when they will take part in a tribal fight. Lengths of cane grass are used as arrows and spears, soon to be replaced by real weapons.

Opposite Page: It was the old "Lapuns" who knew how to stay alive on the battlefield. Though many try to pass their techniques onto the young, modern firearms are changing all the rules.

EXTRACTS

OF A TRIBAL FIGHT DOCUMENTARY

For the past week I have been wandering the highlands gathering information for a three hour documentary on tribal fighting. Following are extracts of comments made by those interviewed:

Anna Dopo, widow of John Pokia, killed in a tribal fight raid in the Western Highlands province:

"My husband was about to graduate in law. He never wanted to fight, he didn't know how. He was outside the fighting zone in our house when the raiding party struck. I was in my husband's brother's house when I heard men calling across the valley that he had been shot. They shot him like an animal. After he was dead they shot him at close range and blew his head apart. I didn't want to believe it, I couldn't believe it until I saw his body.

I am one of his two wives and we have three children. We have worked hard selling pigs and potatoes to raise money so he could finish university. He was an educated man and we looked forward to a good life, but now we have nothing. I must wait and see what compensation will be offered. I cannot ask his brother to avenge him but I will tell his sons the name of the clan responsible."

Above: Widow Anna Dopo.

Sir Wamp Wan, leader of numerous tribal battles and possibly the highland's most respected mediator:

"I was responsible for the death of 33 warriors up until the white man came to the highlands. I have not fought in a tribal fight since, except when I used a rifle to shoot six Big Men to demoralise the enemy and bring a fight to a quick end.

I think the government should give me the power needed to mediate in tribal disputes. I have fought in many wars, I know what I am talking about. I am an old man and you young people will be lost when I die because you will not know the traditional ways of solving disputes."

Above: Sir Wamp Wan

Chris Pokia (27), brother of man killed in tribal fight:

"I have been a school teacher for eight years. I am an educated man and I respect the law but I was forced internally to go on a raid after the death of my brother and two uncles. I was full of anger. I saw men dying, crops destroyed and families scattered. My house and trade store was also burnt to the ground. I only went on one raid with an axe and chopped down trees to get it out of my system. Yes, it is true two of the three men who were involved in the death of my brother died about the same time of my raid. But I didn't kill them. I am an educated man.

Traditionally, it is up to the brother of the deceased to marry his wife and take care of her but I already have a wife and two children. This tribal fight has brought me great hardship. Until now I have been willing to fight for my land but if it started again, I would leave. As an educated person, I would be a prime target."

Above: Maria Kalap

Maria Kalap, Simbu Women's Resource Centre:

"The men enjoy fighting and they go off and leave the women and children who live in fear knowing that at any time the opposing clan may strike. There have been four tribal fights in this area (Simbu) during the past six months and we have had many women coming to us for help. To improve the general standard of living, women's groups have been formed to start small scale businesses but the tribal fighting has ruined the programme. We have started poultry farms, sewing centres and bakeries but many of our projects have been damaged by the fighting. Women should play an active part in stopping the fighting by getting the men to use their common sense, mediating with clan leaders or threatening to take the children and leave if their husbands take part. In this country though, that's not easy for a woman to do."

Joe Wemin Bal, Provincial Secretary Simbu Province:

"We have managed to stop the fighting by successfully applying what we call New Guinea law – burning down houses and killing pigs. – and I think people have responded. It is just a short–term way to solve the problem. We don't expect it to solve the fighting completely. On the longer–term we are looking towards economic development to encourage people not to fight and we have started a mediation squad of respected leaders from throughout the province who negotiate with the clan leaders for quick and peaceful settlement. Successful? It has been very successful though just recently we had to sack the Chairman of the mediation squad when widespread tribal fighting broke out in his home area. His house was burnt down."

Police Operations Commander, Simbu Province:

"We burn down their houses to keep them busy. They haven't got time to fight if they are repairing their crops and rebuilding their houses. It may not be the best way, but we have few options and the community expects us to protect them. We go in and give a warning to stop fighting and if they continue, we teach them a lesson. If we are unsuccessful in our search for firearms we confiscate pigs and hold them for ransom until the weapons are handed in. It was the young policemen who killed the pig you saw, and cut it up to divide among them. I got there late and didn't see it. The commander didn't know."

Father Joseph Bisson, Kerepia Catholic Mission

"Even the churches are taking part in the tribal fighting. Pastors have put down bibles for bush knives to go into battle."

Below: Police Commander,
Southern Highlands Province

Provincial Police Commander, Southern Highlands Province:

"People outside the highlands think they understand the fighting situation, but they don't....this tribal fighting business is a fanatic sickness. People have shelter and food, remove these things and you prevent people from further fighting and killing."

Provincial Police Commander again, responding to accusations that police were responsible for burning down 160 houses and 30 trade stores in the Kagul Valley:

"Half the buildings burnt themselves down."

Left: Fidelis Kunamp

Fidelis Kunamp, "Didiman" (agricultural officer):

"Thousands of Kina have been lost in the fighting. Kau Kau (sweet potato), green cabbage and potatoes are these people's staples, and livelihood. More than 100 tons of potatoes – worth up to K400 a ton – were destroyed in raids or have rotted because the road which links the valley to the markets was blockaded for eight months by the fighting. Now there is no money to buy fertilisers and seed. Food is scarce. When the fighting zone was declared women and children shifted 10 kilometres away for safety, placing a great burden on their relatives who barely had enough food for themselves. People in the area became malnourished. Community schools were also closed down."

Bensen Osil, Community Relations Officer Mt Hagen Police:

"Force is not the solution. Police need to work with the community and demonstrate that there are other ways of solving a dispute. It is not easy for me being a community relations officer. I am left to account for what other policemen do."

Below: Police Community Relations Officer Bensen Osil

Right: A real Huli wigman (as opposed to the unreal ones you are likely to meet in the Southern Highlands who aren't wearing bright yellow paint and a hat of human hair.)

Above: Some of the dramatic aerial scenery of the highlands.

Right: What you would hope to see at a wildlife sanctuary. It's a rare sight-a Hornbill with a beak. Sadly, many of these beautiful birds are being killed for their beaks and feathers which are used in traditional highland bilas.

TOURIST

PNG, THE ULTIMATE ADVENTURE HOLIDAY PACKAGE – DANGER, EXCITEMENT, EXOTIC FOODS, TRIBAL FIGHTING AND PRIMITIVE RITUALS. (HUMOUR)

So you're looking for an adventure holiday package with a difference, something with danger and excitement beyond your wildest dreams, primitive ceremonies, exotic foods, and stunning scenery. Well, have we got just the place for you.......

The first day begins at Ela Beach – Port Moresby's Bondi – where you can bath in tepid waters warmed by local effluent. Cured and cooked until you're lobster red, we'll then take you shopping for tacky T-shirts and cheap Chinese imitations at Garden City to see if you can hold onto your handbag while hundreds try and wrestle it from you.

At lunchtime we'll invite you to sample the local cuisine, dough balls dripping with month old cooking oil, lamb cuts your dog wouldn't eat and outdated frozen foods the rest of the world has rejected. Then we'll take you for some bone-jarring four wheel drive excitement – a quick tour of the city. For those with a yearning for real adventure we'll challenge a PMV driver to share any given hundred metre stretch of road and likely find ourselves being shunted into oncoming traffic and choking in clouds of filthy exhaust fumes.

Artists, particularly, will enjoy the tour of the capital's major landmarks which have become tapestries for thousands of graffiti freaks with signatures larger than their works. Finally, we'll round the evening off with an exorbitant dinner and nightlife that will see you yawning 'til morning. We may even squeeze in a nightcap at the bar during which expatriate locals will either totally ignore you or ply you with alcohol and tales of their own self worth.

By the start of day two, it will dawn on you that this is truly the land of the unexpected – particularly when you're hit with the bill for your first night's accommodation.

From the capital, we'll take you on a day trip to one of four picturesque locations – Varirata National Park, Black Beach, Idlers Bay or Crystal Rapids. If it's a Sunday at Virirata you'll see primitive feasting rites born over hundreds of years of practice, where people gorge themselves with fermented elixirs and charred flesh. As the day progresses, sporadic singing and demonstrations of manhood begin. In a common ritual, a fighting zone is established and males are separated into two opposing sides challenging for possession of a pig skin. In the hot sun exertion is rewarded with more euphoric elixir until both sides are barely standing and one is declared the victor. With the advent of darkness, the weary crowd disperses, hoping to survive the day's final challenge – the drunken drive home.

At 6am the next day we will travel to the airport where – despite confirmed arrival times – we will spend most of the morning waiting for a local flight into the highlands.

Mt Hagen from the sky is picturesque – a patchwork of coffee fields bordered by cloud tipped mountains. You will have every reason to be glad you've landed. In a revealing moment, experienced pilots would tell you that if you can fly in PNG, you can fly anywhere. The conditions are renowned for their treachery – clouds closing in, in front of and behind you, airstrips that end with hundred metre drops and the in-flight service.

Right: The rich culture of the Sepik River attracts tourists from all over the world, most who take so many photographs they can't wait to get home and have them developed so they can see where they have been.

Right: The local marketplace is a fascinating excursion into the day to day life of the Papua New Guinea people. Along the corridors of local produce, babies dangle from rafters in cocoon-like bilums.

Opposite page: The picturesque highlands – a scenic drive made interesting by the likelihood of stumbling into a tribal fight or a compensation claim.

In your two days in the highlands we'll arrange for you to see "a real Huli Wigman" (as opposed to the unreal ones without the costumes), tour a local market and visit a wildlife sanctuary. There is a highway linking the highland provinces so we'll spend a day driving around avoiding pigs and roadblocks – both of which can be fatal if you run into them. We may become caught in a compensation claim or a tribal fight. In the old days the latter rarely presented much of a threat to tourists as arrows were unlikely to reach a distant target. Nowadays, however, it's all front line stuff as high powered rifles are capable of knocking you off your perch at virtually any distance.

Ending each night you can sit back with friends after another exorbitant dinner and sample PNG's famous export crop – not coffee dummy, Spak Brus (Marijuana).

From the highlands, we'll journey to the Sepik and one of the world's most prolific artifact centres where natives carve grotesque aberrations of the spirit world to haunt you to your dying day. Cannibals used to run rampant around the area but today mosquitoes barely leave enough flesh on human bones for them to survive.

By this time your adventure in Papua New Guinea is coming to an end and if things have worked out as planned you will have been robbed, beaten, burgled, shot, stabbed, poisoned, stoned, sunk, shaken and separated from anything of value you brought into the country.

Despite it all, however, it's likely you have survived....... and what a story you'll be taking home.

WORKING IN PORT MORESBY

THE DRAWBACKS – THE BENEFITS
THE MONEY – THE POWER – THE TRUTH

Why do expatriates choose to work in a city where they have to be constantly mindful of their own safety; where they have to live inside homes with barred windows and doors, towering walls and razor wire; where women can't walk the streets by day let alone at night without feeling anxious about their personal security; where husbands and fathers have to be constantly aware of the potential danger to their wives and daughters?

Why work in a city that has one of the highest costs of living in the world; where you pay three dollars for a litre of milk, six dollars for a lettuce and more than $600 a week for what is considered a basic standard of accommodation? What is it about Port Moresby that attracts foreigners to work here?

According to many, the answer is simple – money and power.

Generally speaking expatriates working in either the private or public sector can expect to earn and save money far in excess of what they would obtain in their country of origin. As a rule, says one accountancy firm, middle management staff and higher receive the equivalent in kina to what they earn in dollars back in Australia. In simple terms, that represents almost a 25% increase in pay.

As a further sweetener, employees pay only 2% tax on 25% of their income provided they place it in a gratuity account until the end of their contract and can invest a further 15% of their salary tax free in an interest bearing, offshore superannuation scheme.

And then there is the accommodation component which employers reluctantly accept as a standard part of any executive expatriate package as few will work here without it. Accommodation costs vary but $20,000pa is about where it starts. Though it is not realistic to build that figure in as part of your earnings, it is a saving in that it's not the regular deduction in rental or repayments you were making back in Australia.

Finally, there are the special allowances such as the international market allowance typical of government contracts, and security allowances offered by resource development companies, which can add thousands to your annual savings.

Coupled with the financial benefits, is the power and associated prestige that often comes with working in a developing country, a power that can elevate the mediocre to the status of the mighty. As both business and bureaucracy in Papua New Guinea are still very much in their infancy, expatriates arriving here with what many would consider little more than an average degree of experience or knowledge, find themselves very much in demand; big fish in a small pond. Basic organisation and management skills, motivation and reliability are instantly rewarded. Those responsible for consecutive success are rapidly elevated to positions of staggering influence. Graduate accountants or lawyers find themselves in a position to influence national financing or policy decisions, employees with limited management talents are placed in charge of whole departments, skilled workers become supervisors over an army of labourers.

Left & Below: Port Moresby – a city of contrast. It's said that most expatriates who stay here are either missionaries, mercenaries or misfits. The missionaries give, the mercenaries take and the misfits have no choice but to stay.

For the opportunist, there is a wealth of experience to be gained, which, if used wisely, makes for an impressive resume when it's time to return home.

Many could argue there are a host of other attractions to working in Port Moresby – the professional challenge, an opportunity to experience a new culture, and the chance to make a contribution to a developing country, to name but a few. However, few would truthfully deny the attraction to the benefits mentioned above.

HEAD-HUNTING

THE DILEMMA – THE CURE – IT TAKES PATIENCE – PRIDE AND JOY – CREDIT

So you fancy yourself as a head-hunter and want to know how to cure a head to show off to friends? You can't find the right book, haven't the time to do a course and you've got just the person in mind but are not quite sure how to go about the whole thing.

It's a common predicament.

Assuming you have already taken that first big step (razor sharp bamboo knives used to do the job), the next thing to do is hang the head on a pole until it's in an advanced state of decomposition. If you plan to leave it in a place where everyone can see it, be careful to hang it high enough that inquisitive children can't get their hands on it and make sure it's beyond the reach of domestic pets.

Once you take it down things get a bit tricky and you're best to call on the services of an "Aramabtis" or embalmer (Try the Human Resource section of the Yellow Pages). In the event you can't get hold of one, however, read the following instructions carefully.

First pluck out all the hair and then remove the skin by making a cut from the nape of the neck to the centre of the scalp. Peel the flesh from the skull as you would the skin of a mango and then place it in the sun to dry. In the meantime, take the skull and scrape off the clinging bits of flesh (it's time-consuming, but well worth the effort). You may have trouble emptying the brain from the cavity. If so, use your mouth and teeth to suck it out. Then leave the skull and the skin in a safe place overnight.

By morning (resist the temptation to begin early) fill the skull with mud and insert a bamboo frame to strengthen it and maintain the profile. The bamboo should run from the base of the skull, across the top to meet an artificial lower jaw also made from bamboo.

With the frame in place, pick up the skin, which should now be fairly dry, and draw it back over the skull. You will notice the skin is a little large but it's nothing to worry about. Once everything is properly aligned, take some dried grass and carefully stuff it in between the skull and the skin. (The skin is fairly tough so don't be too concerned about tearing it). Allow the mud time to percolate, which is what prevents further decomposition. Satisfied that everything is in order, use a piece of bone or needle and a robust piece of thread or reed to sew up the original cut at the back of the head.

Throughout this entire process take particular care not to damage the ears and the nose. They should remain in perfect condition and be a lasting clue to the identity of the subject. (There's nothing worse than people not recognising the head with which you have taken so much care). Finally, sew up the mouth and eyes and then smoke the head over a fire for two days before hanging it from your front door for all to admire. (If you want to be arty, you can hang a few beads and some feathers around it.)

NEXT WEEK:

CANNIBALISM. What to do with the rest of that unwanted body.

NOTE: The basis of this story was extracted from the observations of Kiap author Jack Hides who witnessed the preparation of skulls by head-hunters in the early 1900's.

Opposite Page: Though head-hunting in Papua New Guinea has long been outlawed, it is sights such as these that make you wonder how difficult it must have been to keep your head attached to your shoulders in the old days.

RASCAL PROJECT

THE GANG LEADER – WANTING WORK – SAY IT DON'T SPRAY IT – SAD ENDING – GLIMMER OF LIGHT

It was hard to believe the band of youths squatting in front of me were typical of the rascals that roamed the suburbs of Port Moresby at night. They were kids – 10 to 16 years old – scruffy and barefoot; pushing at one another with boisterous bravado as they settled on the ground. It would have been easier to picture them rummaging for a football or playing at school, rather than cutting their way through fences and breaking into houses armed with guns and knives.

Two weeks earlier, the group's leader Ben, had come to our office to ask for assistance for "his boys" – the June Valley Gang from the Tokorara area. They had grown frustrated by government promises to help them and had heard the Foundation was working with youth groups." We don't want to break the law. We just want to work," he said.

Unlike the rest of his gang, Ben was older, maybe in his late twenties. He was short with a wiry build, wearing torn jeans, a dark blue jumper and an expression that conveyed a suspicion and distrust born from years of hardship and struggle. Particularly unsettling were his cold, almost predatory, eyes. While curious faces turned away at my attention, Ben's gaze met me with blatant defiance. This was his home ground. These were his boys.

At our suggestion, the rascal gang had spent a week thinking of ways they could earn money and eventually settled on three suggestions. They would start a bottle collecting business, if we provided a truck; they were prepared to print T–shirts, provided we bought them the press and shirts; they would screen videos in the settlements and charge 20 toea a show – once again – if we gave them a video player and a television set.

For about three hours we sat and considered the options. We talked about the cost of buying the truck, the printing press and the television. We told them we did not have that sort of money but maybe we could work together to raise it. We looked at the maintenance involved in the suggestions, the hours that would need to be worked, the commitment and organisation involved, and whether the money generated would be worth the effort. At every turn they worked out for themselves the difficulties inherent in their propositions, until eventually they arrived at the same point: "So what can we do then?"

What was needed was a short–term project that would involve about 30 youths. It had to be cheap to run and easy to manage with an achievable goal and fair reward. The Foundation's resources were limited. We did not want to get too involved, as providing work for youth groups was not our role, however, we thought it important to demonstrate to the community that youths – even a known rascal group – will work if given direction and encouragement.

"It's the same old story," they said, "everything comes down to money."

Then, a spark: "What about painting over graffiti on the walls of public places?"

The boys looked at each other. "Sure, we can paint but what about the paint and brushes?"

"Well, the Foundation could approach business houses to supply the paints and materials. The NCDIC (City Council) may be willing to provide the transport, and the Department of Youth might even fund the project. It would be a pilot project, lasting maybe two weeks, but it would be a start," we said. Excitement swept the gathering.

Details still had to be worked out. We needed to reach an understanding about what was involved and how everyone was to play their part. It was made clear that the success of the programme depended on our ability to work together. They would have to be ready to work at a particular time every day, 40 hours a week, and if the job wasn't done properly they simply wouldn't be paid. It was all agreed. A working committee was also established to liaise with the Foundation. "This is how government works, but on a smaller scale" we said. "Four youths should be elected to represent 30 and speak on your behalf and in your interests. One of them will be the leader and the four will be expected to arrive at our office at 8am, Wednesday next week to work through the details if you all decide to go through with it. In the meantime, we'll contact the other places to see about the assistance.

The next week four of them turned up early – Ben, the elected leader, his "general" and two others. In the course of the meeting further emphasis was focused on the responsibility the group would be taking on. The Foundation would work with the media to publicize the project. If they did not fulfil their responsibility it would reflect on young people around the nation. Understood.

As the meeting closed Ben and I agreed that as "leaders" of our respective groups we would be singularly answerable to one another. If his boys let us down I would expect him to account for it. Likewise, if the Foundation fell short of its promises he would seek me. (A bit of a worry I thought in hindsight).

As we all parted apparently satisfied with the progress Ben turned secretly and asked me if he could borrow K10 to get him and his boys back to the settlement. It was one of those awkward situations where he appeared to be testing me and I was torn between assuring him of our intentions and the possibility of sacrificing a principle. (It was difficult to overlook the fact that here I was about to "lend" 10K kina to a person who makes a living from robbing people.) Still, I handed him the money. "Ben this is my money, from my own pocket. It's not the Foundation's. I'll lend it to you on your personal assurance that you will give it back to me. I trust you and I leave you to return it," I concluded. The cold eyes did not flinch. "Sure," he said and took the money.

By next week it was all happening. Burns Philp had supplied the paints, the City Council had provided transportation and the Department of Youth were prepared to part with K200 as its contribution to a youth project. The media gave the project extensive publicity – the front page of all three papers plus television and radio. The Justice Minister was the star attraction, sweeping policy and planning aside to don a T–shirt emblazoned with the words "Say it, Don't spray it." Even a small shop owner came to the party with free bottles of Coke for all the youths involved.

At the end of the week Ela Beach was spotless, as were scores of shop fronts. The general public was also showing its support in the editorial pages of the newspapers. But then problems. On the third day of week two, the truck that was to transport them broke down. That afternoon 10 of them turned up at the offices irate and demanding an explanation. We had the assurance of the Council it would be there we said. "Didn't matter" came the reply. "We want transport now. My boys are angry," said Ben.

For about half an hour we tried to work through the situation but it was only with the assurance that the truck would be there tomorrow and our offer to take them back to the settlement in the Foundation vehicle that placated the gang. It was concerning that they were so unreasonable.

What the Foundation was offering them was being perceived as a right; they demanded it. If it had been a larger group and a problem not so easily remedied, it could have easily got out of control.

The two weeks rolled on until the work was done and once again about 10 of them appeared at the office, only they were drunk and demanding money. It was unfortunate that the project's completion corresponded with a government payday, generally regarded as a time to stay indoors as many people wander the streets drunk. Ten of the youths – including Ben –arrived at the office demanding to be paid. I said they were drunk and was concerned the money would only be spent on more grog. "But what about using this money for one of the bigger projects we talked about. This was the start remember?" They were not interested. Pay us, we have worked for it and we want it now," they said.

By this stage my office staff was concerned the gang might wreck the office if they were not paid. "I'll write you a cheque which you can cash on Monday," I said. No, we want the cash now they replied. The scene had grown tense. Ben's eyes once again drew cold.

"O.K I will pay the money, but not to just you and not now. I will pay all 30 of you together at your settlement at Tokokara in one hour's time. You have all done your job well and we will pay you for your effort as agreed ....but it will be at Tokorara.

Unprepared for a compromise, they left.

An hour later I arrived to a group of about 20 boys. Some who were drunk at the office were not there, most who were sober had turned up. Once again, Ben demanded the money and I addressed the group, telling them how happy everyone was with the job the Tokorara youths had done. I talked about how we had worked together and successfully completed a project and then I presented Ben with the cheque saying that it was now his responsibility as a leader to divide their money accordingly. Once again, he said he wanted cash but his plea did not have the same support it had in the office. "You have all done the right thing by us now we are doing the right thing by you," I said. On Monday, you will all have the money you have worked hard for and what you do with it is up to you. We can only hope, however, it is not used to buy more alcohol because the next day you'll be no better off than you were when you first asked the Foundation for help."

With that, I thanked them and said that if they wanted to use that money to seed another project we would again be prepared to assist. Then I left.

It was the last time I saw the June Valley boys.

NOTE: It is now three months after the Graffiti project and I am preparing to go finish. Today there was a knock at the office door. It was Ben who said he had heard I was going and wanted to say he and the boys were sorry to hear the news. We talked for about five minutes, deliberately avoiding mention of the project until he stood to leave. But before he left he turned and shook my hand .... leaving in my palm the 10K note.

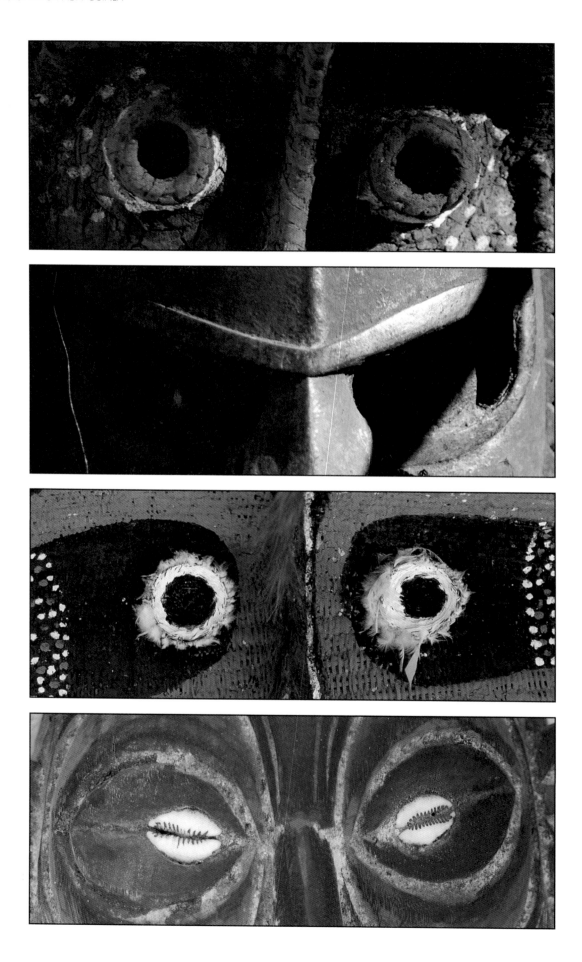

ARTIFACTS

JOE CHAN – PREDICTABLE MARKET –
THE APPEAL – SMUGGLERS – DYING ART

"If I think the artifact means more to them than it's worth to me I tell them to keep it," – Joe Chan.

Like one of his Sepik totems, Joe Chan sits patiently in the extended doorway of his showroom warehouse waiting for the tourist bus to arrive. The bus is carrying a cargo of Japanese businessmen so he's happy – they spend more.

Joe has been in the artifact business for more than 15 years and appears to have the market pretty well worked out. To talk to him you feel he knows the spending patterns of his visitors as well as the artifacts in which he deals. "If they are over 50, they buy small and shiny. Japanese spend the most – generally buying what their tour leaders recommend, while Australians and New Zealanders procrastinate a lot but buy little. As a rule, if it's decorative, has a pig's tusk and has some feathers or rope dangling from it, it's a definite seller," he says, hinting at a commercial savvy long attributed to a Chinese parenthood.

It's only a matter of time before most people interested in Papua New Guinea artifacts arrive at PNG Arts – a warehouse crammed with ancient and modern art. Past the row of towering Sepik totems are corridors of artifacts– intricately carved storyboards and ghoulish spirit masks from the rich middle Sepik area, smoke blackened weaponry and feathered Bilas from the highland provinces, ornaments and musical instruments from the islands and coastal areas. To the layman, it's a fascinating excursion into the creativity and workmanship of the Papua New Guinea people and a unique insight into the important role art plays in their religious and cultural beliefs.

Joe Chan was a panel beater and spray painter before he decided to turn his hobby into a business in 1977. Born in Rabaul and educated in Australia, he recognised the growing worldwide interest in primitive art and while most people were coming and going with whatever they could carry under their arms, Joe was establishing a national network of local suppliers. Today he owns arguably the largest artifact export business in the Pacific, supplying directly to Japan, America and Europe and providing for a thriving local market in Papua New Guinea.

Joe attributes the popularity of the country's art to its cultural and spiritual significance, the quality of the workmanship and the tremendous diversity of the work. "Every village has a distinct style. It may be a pattern, a method of carving or the subject matter, but it is unique to that particular village and no other clan is allowed to copy it," he says.

"The local people are very proud of their work. It's a part of their tradition and they guard it fiercely. A neighbouring village that even comes close to duplicating another village's work would be criticised – sometimes to a point of having to pay compensation," he adds.

Joe says that regardless of whether tourists existed or not, village people would still produce their art, as it remains an important part of the ceremonies they perform in daily life. "In places like the Sepik the artists may be influenced by tourist demand but their basic styles remain in keeping with ancient tradition. To the potential buyer there is an obvious attraction in owning a piece of art which you know has been used in a ceremony practised for hundreds of years," he says.

As a member of The Friends of the Museum, Joe is conscious of the

Above: Joe Chan, artifact dealer. "If it's decorative, has a pig's tusk and has some feathers or rope dangling from it, it's a definite seller."

Opposite page: The artifacts of PNG provide a fascinating excursion into the imagination and skills of their craftsmen. It is unfortunate many of the traditional characteristics of the craft are being lost to future generations unable to recognise their worth.

Above: Says Joe Chan, "Only a small percent of my customers know about the art they purchase. I guess, as a rule, anyone who spends more than K500 has a fair idea about what they are buying but that would only be about 20% of the people who come here."

smuggling of rare works of art out of the country, though he concedes there is little he can do about it apart from report it to the Museum which is likely – at best – to blacklist the offender from entering the country. It is illegal to export PNG artifacts made prior to 1968.

He points out, however, that few very rare pieces of art are left and that the value of those that remain is well known by the people who own them.

"Modern communication has reduced the likelihood of rare artifacts being smuggled out of the country," says Joe.

"Anthropologists working with the National Museum go into the field and identify rare pieces of art with cultural significance. They record their existence with the museum and emphasize to the local community their value. If a particular item was highly prized, its disappearance would be known by the entire community. Gone are the days where the simple village people are exploited for their cultural treasures. Today they know exactly what they are selling. It's the tourists who are the suckers if they think they have bought something rare and valuable for next to nothing!"

Joe attributes the success of his business largely to his relationship with the village people, many with whom he has remained friends since he began collecting artifacts in the 1960's.

"The people in the village have a tremendous appreciation of the simple things in life which I admire," he says.

"They treat me with the same honesty and respect that I show them. If I think a particular item means more to them than it is worth to me, I will tell them to keep it. There is always the thought that if I don't buy it someone else will, but giving it back makes me feel good. I don't need the money that much."

"In Papua New Guinea art dealers come and go, some offering to pay more for what they buy and if the village people want to sell to them I say go ahead. But at the end of the day if things don't work out, they know I'll still be around. I think most of the people I buy from realize I'm here to stay."

According to Joe, Papua New Guinea artifacts are becoming increasingly popular, particularly in Europe, America and, more recently, Japan.

"European and American markets have traditionally had a high regard

for PNG art but recently the Japanese have become the biggest buyers," he says.

"They buy at two levels; tourists who buy handfuls of small gifts for family and friends, and Japanese museums that have a lot of money to spend and are building up their collections. The Australian and New Zealand markets are also showing greater interest, possibly pushed along by the recent demand for Aboriginal art."

Joe says buyers of PNG artifacts fall into four distinct categories – dealers, collectors, businessmen and tourists. The dealers know what they want and buy in bulk to meet the needs of their own local markets while the collectors tend to specialise in a particular item such as Bilum (string) bags or masks. Businessmen look for what they have heard is rare and valuable but tend to know little about the subject. The item will generally be portable and decorative, something to hang in the office. And finally, there are the tourists who, like tourists anywhere else in the world, want everything for nothing and generally settle on a modest souvenir of their visit.

"Only a small percent of my customers knows a lot about the art they purchase. They tend to buy what appeals to them at the time. As a rule I guess anyone who spends more than K500 has a fair idea about what they are buying but that would only be about 20% of the people who come in here," says Joe.

Asked if he feels confident about the future of PNG's artifact industry, Joe says he is concerned." A lot of the young people are moving out of the villages and heading for the towns so the knowledge and skills of the old artists are not being passed down. Much of the traditional learning in Papua New Guinea is passed on through experience and direct contact between one generation and the next but there are fewer young people left in the village to pass the knowledge on to. Sadly, as a result, the art is slowly losing its richness," he says.

.....a prospect he points out that should concern us all.

Above: The local people are very proud of their work. It's a part of their tradition and they guard it fiercely. A neighbouring village that even comes close to duplicating another village's work would be heavily criticised - sometimes to the point of having to pay compensation.

IMAGINE

ATTACKED – BLINDED – ABDUCTED – ROLLOVER – STALKED – MESSAGE – REASON

Imagine you are coming home from a dinner party at about 10 o'clock. It's been a long day, but an enjoyable evening. You are relaxed – the wine was good – and you're reliving some of the more memorable moments of the dinner. Rounding the corner with your house in the distance, you activate the electronic gate and sidle towards the opening, change down a gear and prepare to make the ascent up the drive.

Suddenly the door flies open and you are yanked violently from your car. There is an explosion of pain in the back of your head that sends you reeling to the ground. As you fall sideways with the momentum of the blow, two men in masks grab your arms and jerk your head back. Panic floods your system. Suddenly your eyes are burning with a searing, excruciating pain. You are on your knees screaming, blinded, but the violence hasn't stopped. More voices, more pain. They are viciously kicking and beating you, using wood and chains. Confusion. Too many of them. You raise your arm to try and cover your face and reach your eyes but the reflex meets with a blunt, crushing force and the rain of blows continues.

Suddenly you are stood up, pushed forward and bundled into the back seat of your car. Your head crashes against a metal panel as you fall back and are wedged on the ground between the front and the back seat. You are pawing at your eyes still trying to stop the burning and for a moment the barrage of punches subsides – but only long enough for you to realise the ordeal is not over. Two men clamber into the back pushing on top of you and again hitting you around the head and kicking you. A knee crashes down onto your chest, the weight of a body forcing the air from your lungs. More pain. You're straining to breathe.

It's all happening so fast but amid the confusion dawns the realisation of what is going on. A single question repeats itself. *Where are they taking me?* You hear laughter, the laughter of your assailants. Tyres are screeching, the car is lunging forward, jerking, swaying, accelerating – painfully. *God the pain. How much longer?*

Impressions of fleeting light flash down at you through the haze of darkness. You can still barely open your eyes and are pinned between the seats. The driver is shouting at the rest of them in local language. They are shouting back – urgent, excited voices. The violence is now random and for the first time you feel the warmth of your own blood streaming down your face. You begin to acknowledge the injury you have suffered and the fear that is welling inside you. *What do they plan to do with me? Will they kill me? How can I escape?*

As if the thought was spoken, a fist crashes down on the back of your neck.

From the floor of the car you are wrenched upwards and slumped into a corner of the back seat. Once again fists strike at your body and voices jeer at you, taunting you to resist or try and make a break. You are pulled towards the man next to you. You can't see him, your eyes still throb with the pain and everything is a blur, but you can feel his closeness, the smell of beer on his breath, the perspiration of his body, the aggression in his voice. He is yelling at you –inches from your face – pulling you around by the collar of your shirt. Angry. There is laughter in the car, then pain as he swats you back into the corner.

The car pulls up amid the shouting and excitement of more people. Bodies clamouring around the car window. The distant door is opened and you feel temporary relief from the crushing presence next to you. But it is temporary. More bodies pile in. They take it in turns to beat you.

It goes on for hours. Several stops are made at different places and each time, the same thing – poking, prodding, punching and laughter. *Must escape !*

Then the fleeting impressions of light stop and the car is accelerating rapidly through the darkness. A new type of laughter sweeps the car, an excited, almost hysterical laughter. The car is travelling out of the city along the highway. The man next to you wrenches you forward and tells you to drink from a empty bottle of beer into which he has just urinated. You dry retch. Do it, he commands. But you turn away and once again he strikes you in the back of the head and forces you back to the floor. As the car speeds forward, the fear mounts and for the first time you think *This is it, I am going to die.* Again, the person next to you pulls you up, only this time he has his pants down and wants you to use your mouth on him. Again you turn away. He says he has a knife, threatens to use it if you don't do as he says, but despite the pain you resist. You feel movement and brace yourself for the blow. The blade pierces your lower back. You scream in pain. "Do it," he roars......

Suddenly, the car is screeching and swerving wildly out of control. You feel the vehicle lift and flip into the air, tensing in anticipation of the impending impact. There is a cacophony of noise, the crashing of metal on earth, glass shattering. Everything is spinning. The roof of the car is torn off by the force of the landing and you are hurled into the air away from the vehicle. You have landed in reeds and water. From the darkness you can hear voices searching for you, irritated, angry voices. You lay still, waiting, hoping, they will leave. The water has brought some relief to your eyes but it is stinging the wound in your back and your ribs are throbbing. You ache all over and have trouble concentrating. *Keep still, block out the pain. Don't move until after they have gone.* Darkness envelopes your mind.

When you wake they are gone. You have no idea of how long you have been unconscious but it is still dark and you can barely move. In the moonlight you can make out the car. Its headlights are still shining underneath the water. Agonisingly you climb the bank and walk along the road. You are barefoot – they took your shoes – but you continue to walk. Two cars come towards you from the distance but you hobble quickly into the bushes and hide, fearing they are returning, and struggle on.

Three hours later you stagger into a police station and collapse............

As horrific and barbaric as this story sounds, the most disturbing point is that it actually happened, and to a friend of mine.

Rod Miller was in a satisfactory condition when I visited him in hospital today. Despite the trauma, he says he is angry but mostly saddened by what has happened." Remarkably, even as I lay wedged in the back of the car I couldn't help thinking this wasn't their fault, they are just frustrated kids," he said.

Informed opinion suggests Rod was abducted as part of a rascal recruitment drive aimed at impressing potential gang members. A vendetta aimed at Rod has been discounted. Police are questioning one of the men believed to be involved – a 19 year old they found at the site of the accident. It seems likely the other three will be caught – though for how long, no one is confident.

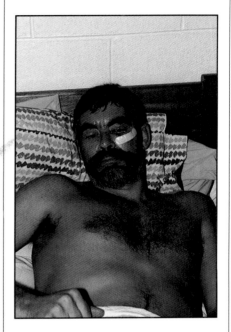

Above: Rod Miller in hospital after his ordeal. He was abducted by rascals in his own car while waiting for the electronic gate to open to his house. As he said, he only dropped his guard for a minute. It was enough.

THE SNAKE MAN

IN SEARCH OF SERPENTS – PNG THE LAST FRONTIER – TOKEN TATTOO – RESEARCH

The Motu people of the Central Province call him Gai Gai Tauna – the Snake Man.

Mark O'Shea (34) wandered six continents searching for snakes in the name of research before arriving in Papua New Guinea to photograph, scale, milk and release its most venomous serpents. He's been bitten more times than he cares to remember (though only six times by snakes that kill people) and in the process has temporarily lost his eyesight, been partially paralysed, and had his chest muscles contract to a point where he could barely breathe. His worldwide search has also seen him bitten four times by deadly spiders, wrestling with a South American Anaconda and being stalked by a jaguar, all of which he dismisses simply as "an occupational hazard."

As the world's so-called last great frontier, Papua New Guinea attracts experts and "ologists" from all over the world – anthropologists, geologists, biologists, sociologists and – according to Gai Gai's business card – even freelance herpetologists (people who study reptiles and amphibians.)

As you might expect from someone whose entire reason for being, appears to be crawling around in long grass at night in search of snakes, Gai Gai has an air of eccentricity about him. The impression looms at first meeting with the sight of him in his jungle greens and T-shirt emblazoned with the image of a Cobra and some reference to an international snake convention. His T-shirt is rolled to the shoulder, revealing a primitive snake tattoo; his pants are secured to his slight frame by a garish silver belt buckle, also shaped in the image of a serpent.

In keeping with his Irish lineage, Gai Gai has fiery red hair and a beard that threatens to overrun his pallid complexion. His crowning glory is a well-worn slouch hat with a smell that gives credence to a later boast that it makes a great receptacle for holding reptiles.

Our conversation gets off to a slow start as he is ill at ease with pleasantries, weaving in and out of the conversation with feigned interest until he's eventually drawn out by the mention of reptiles.

Suddenly we are evolving through the 65 million year history of snakes and his fascination with an animal that is technically deaf, has no arms or legs and yet has still managed to become such an efficient predator. He is talking about some 5,700 different species of snakes and lizards in scientific words that were undoubtedly longer than the snakes to which they referred. There was his work as a fellow with the Royal Geographical Society in the Amazon Basin, his exploits in Honduras, Africa and Borneo and some interesting serpent snippets. Did you know that women in the Western Province lactate into fresh water to attract and catch snakes to eat ? Have you heard about the unwitting carnivorous pythons? They don't mean to be cannibalistic. Two pythons coming from different directions stumble across food and start slowly eating it, one from each end. Only once eating begins, everything goes onto automatic with eyes raised to the heavens in ecstasy until suddenly one's eating away when the lights go out. There was also the yarn about people who have been killed by the head of a snake decapitated hours earlier when a particular nerve was triggered that clamps the jaw and releases the fatal venom. ("C'mon Joe, dying from poison looks nothing like that. What a card!").

.......which was about when we got onto what he was actually doing here. In short, Gai Gai has spent the past six months running around PNG collecting venomous snakes for the Liverpool School of Tropical Medicine in England. He measures, weighs, milks, photographs then releases all of those he catches with the exception of venomous species which he sends back to England for antivenene research.

"There is nothing I would prefer to be doing. A bad day for me is going 24 hours without having sighted a snake," he says.

"There are more than 60 species of land snakes in Papua New Guinea of which 26 are venomous, but only seven are dangerous to man. I have managed to catch 23 species this visit. It's not easy to find them as they tend to live in dark places like piles of coconut husks or in dead trees. Out towards Brown River or along the road to Sogeri at night after a downpour you'll always see a few."

"I have been called to villages many times to get rid of dangerous snakes. One Motuan community (the one that calls him Gai Gai) wanted to reward me by tattooing a large snake on my arm for removing a deadly Black Snake from the school latrine. It sounded like a good idea at first –like Christina Dodwell with the crocodile ceremony – but they wanted to do my whole arm so I decided to give it a miss. They did a small snake on my shoulder instead.

"Generally Papua New Guineans are fascinated by what I do, although many of them think I'm crazy, not just for collecting them, but for letting them go afterwards. I stayed in one village and collected a large sack of snakes. Everyone thought it was great and expected a big feed when all the work was done so I had to sneak out the back and let them all go. When they asked me to explain what I had done I told them the snakes and I have an understanding – they don't bite me, as long as I don't bite them."

Above: As you might expect from someone whose entire reason for being appears to be crawling around in long grass at night in search of snakes, Gai Gai (pictured) has an air of eccentricity about him.

FELICIA

BACK TO THE VILLAGE – HARDSHIP IN LAE – VEIFFA – A QUESTION FOR THE YOUNG

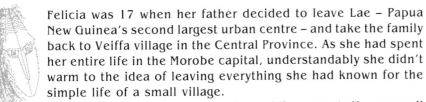

Felicia was 17 when her father decided to leave Lae – Papua New Guinea's second largest urban centre – and take the family back to Veiffa village in the Central Province. As she had spent her entire life in the Morobe capital, understandably she didn't warm to the idea of leaving everything she had known for the simple life of a small village.

At the time, Felicia's father was a senior public servant. He was well paid, living in a house with his own car but didn't like the way Lae was developing with its escalating crime and increasing hardship. He believed it wasn't a healthy environment for his family to grow up in so he left, taking with him his wife, Felicia and her younger sister. As Felicia said, it was a traumatic break. "I didn't want to leave Lae but I wanted to be with my family."

Seven years have now passed since Felicia returned to her village and her attitude provides an interesting insight into what could be a solution to Papua New Guinea's law and order problem, contributed to by the increasing numbers of disillusioned youth who are turning to crime in the urban centres.

Now when Felicia talks about Lae she thinks of hardship. She talks of having to live in cramped conditions, of being hungry and surrounded by people constantly complaining about their lot in life. She talks of how difficult it was for the family to make ends meet and how she always wanted things she couldn't have – new clothing, money to go out, special foods and television. And of course there was the crime problem. A young girl couldn't walk the streets alone without fearing for her safety even in the day, let alone the night.

In contrast she says Veiffa has everything. "Here we never go hungry. We have fruit, vegetables and meats, enough to easily feed the whole village. If we want to we can eat five meals a day. We have clean water from tanks or the nearby river and there is always something to do and plenty of time to relax. In the village everyone knows everybody and they help each other. It is a good community and you can walk at any hour of the night without feeling it's dangerous."

"Sure there are some things I miss about the city, but Port Moresby is only a few hours away and I can still go there if I want to visit. But it will always be just to visit. This is my home. I look at all the problems in the city and I'm glad I'm here. I can't understand why young people are leaving their villages for the city. It just doesn't make sense."

Opposite Page: "Life in the village is simple. If we wanted to we could have five meals a day. There is always something to do and plenty of time to relax."

– SNIPPETS –

- "Where else in the world can you overtake a policeman at 100mph and have him wave at you as you go by."
- Following a spate of armed hold–ups in and around Lae, two drivers of a security van decided to chuck a swifty and steal K600, claiming they had been held up by bandits. They called police to the scene to tell their story but police discovered the money. Where? Possibly buried in the bush or hidden in their village I hear you say? Not quite. They found the money under the driver's seat.
- "There are only three types of expatriates in this country – missionaries, mercenaries and misfits."
- A Chimbu woman was admitted to hospital with axe wounds received in a clan fight following a compensation dispute with a Goroka man. The man was accidentally struck by a missile from a small child's catapult.
- In the snippets column of Papua New Guinea's leading newspaper: Q: What do Cannibals eat? A: Baked Beings.
- ".......The rascals also took my microwave but I'll probably get it back when they realise they can't get a picture on it. "
- " We use the back stitch method to train staff – one stitch forward and two stitches back."
- A man was shot dead and seven others were seriously injured after an argument over a pancake erupted into a major fight in the Western Highlands at the weekend. – Story: Post Courier.
- The theft of a chicken at a freezer store led to a dangerous street riot near the main Lae market yesterday with seven injured and hundreds of kina of damage to property. – Story: Post Courier.
- "Have you heard how disappointed the Chimbu woman was when she discovered that the 21 inch National was actually a television set."
- A highland police Commander has alerted motorists about rascals who are laying on the road and pretending they are injured. His warning followed an incident where he nearly ran over two people believed to be part of an ambush. In his own words he told reporters: "Last night I was driving home very fast at about 140kmph since there was little traffic at the time and I also wanted to get home and have some sleep when..........."
- Members of a cargo cult in New Ireland have refused to allow any census work in their village, saying they have already sent their names to the United States of America at the request of the US President – Post Courier.
- Police HQ despatched telexes to provincial commands telling police to be on the lookout for a stolen yacht. Mt Hagen police responded: Searched entire Waghi River. No such yacht sighted.
- "I'm a bit worried about the effects Circus Bruno will have in the highlands – especially the act where the magician saws the woman in half. I've got this vision of hundreds of highlanders taking their wives home to try the same trick."
- A man driving a Range Rover was pleased when three youths came to his assistance to fix his flat tyre but apparently his gratitude was not enough of a reward. When the job was completed, they took his watch, his wallet and drove off with the car.
- The term "Charismatic" took on a new dimension today when I received a letter from the Charismatic Revival Group of Enga Province demanding the Foundation's attention. The letter said that if financial assistance was not immediately forthcoming the group would "take the law into our own hands by taking physical actions on you."

Below: Visiting the local markets is a great way to spend a Saturday morning. Fresh produce is generally in abundance though you have to be quick as villagers arrive at first light and, like hitting the supermarket at home, if you are not there early you'll get caught in the crowd or simply miss out. At Gordons Market in Port Moresby you'll find a variety of foods including fresh fruits, vegetables, poultry and live turtles.

Right: The markets of Mt Hagen (top) and Rabaul (centre) are possibly the best known for their variety of fruits and vegetables.

THE MARKETS

Left: At the local markets, sleeping babies dangle from the rafters in cocoon - like bilums.

Below: Though some of the fruits and vegetables are well known to expatriates - eg. pineapples, potatoes, mangoes and oranges etc - there are many that are likely to be unknown. An excellent publication for those looking to dabble in the local "Kai Kai" is Kaikai Aniani by R.J May. (Try the University Bookshop or Gordon and Gotch).

LASTING IMPRESSIONS

I have deliberately waited six months after leaving Papua New Guinea to write the final chapter of my book hoping that with the distance of time I'll be able to gather what are truly my lasting impressions of the country.

There are many things that will remain in the forefront of my memories of Papua New Guinea and I am happy to write that most of them are favourable.

As I look back over what I have written and my 18 months in the country, I think of what a fantastic adventure it all was and how distant it all now seems. I think about the constant fascination my surroundings held for me as a point of comparison for everything else I had known; the variety of my experiences; the surprise and unpredictability of every new day.

It is difficult for me to visualise PNG without considering the constant paradox of day to day living in Port Moresby. In the harbour capital, ramshackle communities of corrugated tin and timber form an incongruous backdrop to towering office blocks of reflective glass. In the main street, expatriates struggle from department stores to cars under the weight of plastic bags crammed with household goods, while nationals, standing inside in bare feet, deliberate over brands of tinned fish and dried biscuits. At night, in the hills overlooking the harbour, the gas lamps of squatter settlements burn like dim beacons, surrounded by a constellation of lights from modern apartments. The fascination was not so much in the difference, but the distance between the two cultures and the challenge that lays ahead. For many of the people of Papua New Guinea the transition has already been enormous; from the Stone-age to the Space-age in less than a lifetime.

Of course some of my fondest memories are of the people I met and of the times we shared. It's interesting that my most enjoyable memories relate to the simple pleasures of the times I spent in the villages.

In my position as executive officer of the Foundation of Law Order and Justice, I was often asked to comment on the extent of the country's law and order problem, a subject which forms part of my most lasting impression of PNG. After 18 months of being involved in the effort to improve the situation at a national level, I am left with a mixed sense of apprehension, inevitability and optimism.

Personally, I do not believe the PNG government is capable of containing the law and order problem any more than I believe the Australian government is effectively contributing to averting the anarchy which is likely to occur in the country's primary urban centres within the next 10 years. The administrative infra-structure in PNG is simply not there to ensure adequate management of the law and order process, and with each passing day the situation continues to deteriorate. Sadly, the time has passed when a complete breakdown in government could have been averted through a democratic process. It is now only a matter of time.

The extent of lawlessness in PNG is being determined by a range of factors - not just the government's ability to enforce the law. The country's crime problem is a symptom of economic, cultural and social disharmony, all of which are being exacerbated by nothing more sinister than the country's destiny to become a modern nation. But as the government continues to respond to a range of immediate issues relevant to national

Opposite page: The faces of Papua New Guinea are likely to shape some of my most lasting impressions of the country.

Above: Port Moresby harbour is sprinkled with landmarks, as many on land as in the water. This beached vessel became a playground for children of a nearby village.

Opposite page: My most vivid and pleasurable re-collections of the country will be of the times I spent in the villages.

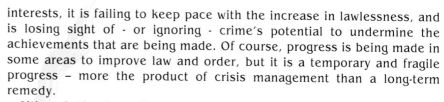

interests, it is failing to keep pace with the increase in lawlessness, and is losing sight of - or ignoring - crime's potential to undermine the achievements that are being made. Of course, progress is being made in some areas to improve law and order, but it is a temporary and fragile progress – more the product of crisis management than a long-term remedy.

Although the Australian government continues to play a key role in efforts to improve the standards of law and order in PNG, my 18 months has left me questioning the value of its contribution - both past and present. What Australia gave the country was a rigid western justice system, which was fair enough given it knew no other system. But what Australia subsequently failed to do, I believe, was assist the PNG government to adapt the western model to the PNG circumstance and build on some of the successful elements of traditional Melanesian law. For example, the Melanesian people have an incredibly strong sense of community and belonging which has evolved over thousands of years. The Wantok system and the bond the people have with their land reflect the prominence both elements play in Melanesian society today. During the past 10 years both the Justice Department and a plethora of authoritative law and order reports - notably that of William Clifford - have identified the potential to harness these traditional elements in a modern campaign to improve law and order. Yet despite continued calls for assistance in areas such as the improvement of the village court system, community policing and probation programs, and law awareness initiatives, the Australian government continues to provide massive funds and expertise only to law enforcement.

Though I accept that the Australian government is led by the priorities of PNG's government of the day, surely it has a responsibility to assess the long-term consequence of its allocations, consider the alternatives and influence future direction. The Australian government's three year aid program to the PNG police force illustrates the point. What is the benefit of pouring millions of Kina into the police department's ability to arrest people when the court system is incapable of processing the number of criminals it has at the moment? And should the court system succeed in prosecuting the criminals, what good is that when the prisons are so dilapidated they are unable to keep existing offenders incarcerated? My point is that these three components of the western justice system - police, courts and correctional services - should be improved in unison, and that they should compliment and strengthen - not replace - a community based justice system sensitive to the Melanesian culture.

I also wonder about the corporate sector's commitment to improving law and order. By now, particularly after Bougainville, business has most certainly realised that its profits are dependent on its ability to curb lawlessness, yet still it is likely to do little to improve the situation beyond keeping its own doorstep clean. In my time, the private sector was certainly given the opportunity to sensibly influence government, yet little was achieved, mainly because representatives failed to understand the government's needs and the problem, let alone the ways of overcoming it. To simply say "we pay our taxes" is not enough and time is making that more and more obvious. Business should be accepting greater responsibility for the circumstances and working with government to develop practical, long-term solutions which are invariably in their mutual interests.

In summary, I have no simple solution to the law and order problem in PNG and I leave it to others to persist with the effort that must be made. But I hasten to add that I remain optimistic about the country's future.

I choose to look at Papua New Guinea in a historical context and consider it with that Melanesian sense of inevitability which I used to mistake for apathy. What PNG is going through at the moment is what countries throughout the world have gone through over thousands of years. Every country has endured similar trials to those now being experienced by Papua New Guinea and every one of them has gone on to become a great nation.

I have no doubt Papua New Guinea will do the same.